JOSE PLEADING WITH CARMEN—ACT IV

Carmen

by

Prosper Mérimée

Translated and Annotated with an Introduction by

Walter F. C. Ade

Purdue University

Barron's Educational Series, Inc.

Woodbury, New York • London • Toronto • Sydney

Illustrations
The cover illustration, frontispiece, and picture on page 28 are from *The Victor Book of the Opera* (New York: Victor Talking Machine Company, 1929).

All inquiries should be addressed to:
Barron's Educational Series, Inc.
113 Crossways Park Drive
Woodbury, New York 11797

Library of Congress Catalog Card No. 75-22471

International Standard Book No. 0-8120-0427-2

Library of Congress Cataloging in Publication Data

Mérimée, Prosper, 1803-1870.
    Carmen.

    Bibliography: p. 98
    I. Ade, Walter Frank Charles. II. Title.
PZ3.M544C25 [PQ2362]   843'.7   75-22471
ISBN 0-8120-0427-2

PRINTED IN THE UNITED STATES OF AMERICA

45   510   98765432

To my son, George Leonard Ade,
a devotee of Bizet's *Carmen*

Contents

The translator and editor, Walter Frank Charles Ade, Ph.D., Ed.D., F.I.A.L., F.I.B.A., has been Professor of Modern Languages and Education at Purdue University since 1959. Before that time he was on the faculties of the University of Toronto, the Lisgar Collegiate Institute, Ottawa, Canada, Valparaiso University, Arizona State University, and in 1955-56 he taught in Bavaria, West Germany, as a Fulbright Professor.

PROSPER MÉRIMÉE

Deveria (1829)

Introduction

Prosper Mérimée:

The Man, the Author, and his *Carmen*

The Life of Prosper Mérimée

Prosper Mérimée, the author of *Carmen*, lived in France during the first seventy years of the tumultuous nineteenth century. He was born during the war-torn days of Napoleon Bonaparte when romanticism was in blossom, lived through its full flowering during the political upheavels of 1830 and 1848, witnessed the literary reaction called realism, and died the very year that Napoleon III waged his ill-starred war against Bismarck's Prussia (1870), when naturalism was becoming the vogue in French literature.

Prosper Mérimée was the son of Jean François Léonor Mérimée, a painter and an art historian, and Anna Moreau, who, like her husband, was an artist. His native city was Paris, where he was born on September 28, 1803. In his youth, Prosper Mérimée was a rather dandified young man, whose admiration for England and things English (particularly for the English writer Hazlitt) was so strong that he actually became an Anglophile. At school in Paris he did not distinguish himself as a brilliant student or as an outstanding young man in any other way, and it was not until he was twenty years of age that he became seriously interested in literature as a career.

Early in 1823 Mérimée made his literary debut with a series of five romantic plays, which he published in 1825 as *The Theatre of Clara Gazul*, pretending that he had translated them from the works of an imaginary Spanish dramatist. Only one of these plays, *The Spaniards in Denmark*, deserves passing mention. The others are rather juvenile and possess little literary merit. In the preface to the collection, Mérimée claims that Clara Gazul had been persecuted in Spain by the Roman Catholic clergy, had taken refuge in England, and had spent her leisure time writing the work. In spite of their weaknesses, these plays nevertheless attracted attention because of their originality. Two years later, Mérimée published a collection of poems entitled *La Guzla*, which purported to be translations from Illyrian (an early Indo-European language), but which in reality were Mérimée's own creations. (It should be noted that the names *Gazul* and *Guzla* are anagrams.)

At this time, Mérimée's intellectual pursuits were so intense that within a few months he was solidly installed in the best literary coteries of Paris. He was a constant *habitué* of these artistic and literary salons and rapidly became a prominent figure in society. In particular, he was one of the regular guests of the beautiful Madame de Récamier, whose salon was especially celebrated in Paris at that time.

During his rapid rise to prominence and popularity in Parisian literary circles, another significant event took place which was an influence throughout the rest of his life. About 1825, Mérimée met and became the intimate friend of Marie-Henri Beyle (1783-1842), better known as Stendhal, his *nom de plume*. Stendhal's theories and temperament exerted a strong and lasting influence on Mérimée, who remained his disciple until Stendhal died in 1842.

It was at this time that the romantic movement in France, under the leadership of Victor Hugo, was filtering down from elite literary circles to the general reading public. Mérimée—originallly one of romanticism's most ardent supporters and a pioneer in the movement in France—lost interest in it.

His next literary work was *The Jacquerie* in 1828, a chronicle play which dealt with the violent and bloody peasant war in the fourteenth century. True to form, Mérimée was minutely exact in historical detail. The following year he published the first of a long line of historical novels, *The Chronicle of the Reign of Charles IX,* in which he treats of the shameful St. Bartholomew's Day Massacre of the French Protestants in 1572. Critics have praised this work as a very fine imitation of the historical manner and style introduced by Sir Walter Scott. Immediately following the completion of this work he wrote a play, *The Fiacre of the Holy Sacrament* (1829); in it he bitterly satirized religious hypocrisy, as Moliére had done in *Tartuffe.* From 1829 to 1830 Mérimée wrote four of his most interesting short stories: *The Etruscan Vase, The Taking of the Redoubt, Mateo Falcone,* and *Tamango.* These, collected with others, were published as *Mosaique* in 1833.

In 1830 Mérimée travelled in Spain, where he met the Countess of Montijo in Madrid, who told him the story of *Carmen.* At this time he also wrote his *Letters from Spain.* While returning through France, the July Revolution of 1830 broke out in Paris, causing Charles X to abdicate and Louis Philippe to ascend the throne. Owing largely to his connections with the Count d'Argout, a statesman in high regard in Louis Philippe's new government, Mérimée entered the French Civil Service and held various public offices. He shifted from department to department until he finally found a post which interested him and for which he was really suited in the Fine Arts Division of the Home Office. During these years he led a dissipated and cynical life and completed little of any real value—only a short novel *The Double Blunder* (1833). In 1835 he was appointed Inspector General of Historical Monuments in France, in which capacity he had to study the ancient monuments, see to it that they were not destroyed or damaged, and, if necessary, restore them as much as possible to their original condition. This work required him to travel throughout France. Mérimée held this post for twenty years and carried out his duties conscientiously and efficiently; as a result of his good

work, he became the founder of the Commission of Historic
Monuments of France. Out of these travels came his *Travel
Notes,* which are charming descriptions of several of his tours of
inspection, entitled *Notes on a Voyage in the South of France*
(1835), *Notes on a Voyage in the West of France* (1836), and
Notes on a Voyage in Auvergne and Limousin (1838).

In 1836 Mérimée began his mysterious *Correspondence
with Another Unknown Lady,* which, since his death, has
created a very lively interest. Major literary works were
produced between 1836 and 1845: *The Venus d'Ille* (1837),
Arsène Guillot (1844), and *Carmen* (1845). In 1840 he undertook
a trip to Corsica, which resulted in his *Notes on a Voyage in
Corsica* (1840) and, more important, in his *Colomba* (1840),
which is considered by many to be his literary masterpiece. His
Carmen, which has been said "to breathe the very air of
Spain," was followed by *A History of Don Pedro I, King of
Castile* (1848) and by a work entitled *The Gypsies* (1852).

For a time Mérimée discontinued writing novels and short
stories, turning rather to historical research, through which he
hoped to become a member of the French Academy. He
published long, dry historical works which are no longer widely
read: *Essay on the Social War* (1841), which was followed by
Studies on Roman History (1844), consisting of three parts: *The
Conspiracy of Catiline, The Social War,* and *Julius Caesar.* He
had completed only the first two of these three parts when, after
violent debate, he was elected to the French Academy on March
14, 1844, succeeding Charles Nodier. (Mérimée had already
been made a member of the Academy of Inscriptions and
Belles-Lettres.) The Revolution of 1848 again made France
temporarily a republic, soon to be succeeded by the Empire of
Napoleon III. During these years Mérimée seems to have
continued to devote his attention almost exclusively to historical
projects, for he produced no works of any real literary
significance. He also travelled widely in Greece and Italy in this
period in order to become more thoroughly acquainted with the
sources of his historical research.

In 1853, the Emperor Napoleon III married Eugénie de

Montijo, the daughter of Mérimée's old and close friend, the Countess of Montijo. Owing to the friendship and influence of the Empress he became closely attached to the court at the Tuileries; indeed, he was actually included as a member of the intimate reunions of the imperial circle and sometimes even dined alone with the royal family. It was at this time that Mérimée handed over the results of his research and his collected notes on Julius Caesar to Napoleon III, who was also writing a *History of Julius Caesar.* In the same year (1853), he was made a senator and sent on various diplomatic missions of a particularly delicate nature. In return for these services, Mérimée was decorated by the Emperor with the Cross of Grand Officer of the Legion of Honor in 1866. At this time he also undertook an extended European tour, visiting Italy, Spain, and particularly England, where he became acquainted with Lord Palmerston and Gladstone.

In the last years of his life Mérimée turned enthusiastically to Russian literature in search of new vistas, and he was the first prominent man of letters in France to introduce some of the works of the best Russian writers into his native land. He translated Turgenev, Gogol, and Pushkin, and was also greatly interested in Russian history. As early as 1852 he wrote *Episode in the History of Russia* and *The Demetrius Pretenders,* and in 1852-53 he translated five selected Russian works by Pushkin and Gogol. In 1855 *The Cossacks of the Ukraine* was published, and in 1865 *The Cossacks of Times Past* appeared. A short time before he died, Mérimée also began a *History of the Reign of Peter the Great*; and among his posthumous writings, which were published in 1873, was *The Pistol Shot,* by Pushkin.

Mérimée's works dealing with Russian history are completely impersonal, dry, cold, and very exact. His translations into French of Russian literary works, however, are excellent. In his remaining few years he wrote his last two *novellas, The Blue Room* (1866) and *Lokis* (1869). Although they are not unworthy of Mérimée, they cannot be classed among his best literary products.

Mérimée's health began to fail and for that reason he often

retreated to Cannes. In 1869 it was rumored that he had died. Although Mérimée was in fact desperately ill, he recovered temporarily to such a degree that he was able to return to Paris. He remained there until the capitulation of Sedan in the Franco-Prussian War. He then went back to Cannes, where he died on September 24, 1870, at the age of sixty-seven.

Mérimée was a man of contradictions. In his works he strove to appear cold, impersonal, and aloof, yet as a friend of the royal family he composed many charades, witty epigrams, and tales for the imperial circle only. He was at home in aristocratic and intellectual gatherings. Brief, curt, and completely objective in his literary style, in the society of his choice he was a brilliant conversationalist and a gallant. He knew many languages, including various Spanish dialects and the language of the Basques. He also spoke the Romany tongue of the Spanish gypsies with considerable fluency. He was, in addition, a great traveller, having traversed the length and breadth of Europe in order to study his subjects at first hand. Critic and courtier, dilettante and diplomat, historian and novelist, antiquarian and statesman, linguist and *littérateur*—Mérimée illustrates admirably the diversity of the French.

Mérimée, disenchanted with the period in which he was living, became a testy old man. He found nothing to interest him in contemporary literature, for his constant idol, Stendhal, had died and Mérimée found no one to replace him. He showed his indebtedness and his loneliness by honoring Stendhal in a *Biography* which was published posthumously in 1874. He felt that Flaubert was "wasting his talent under the pretense of realism" and that Victor Hugo was "a man with the most beautiful figures of speech at his disposal, who did not take the trouble to think but rather intoxicated himself with his own words." Baudelaire's theory, style, and imagery infuriated him, and Renan filled him with contempt and pity. Scornful of contemporary authors and their works, and disgruntled with himself for feeling as he did, Mérimée could no longer settle down to work seriously as he had done before. Thus it was that he died during an era when his popularity had waned with the advance of the times and before his works had become fully recognized as classics.

Romanticism and Mérimée's
Role in the Romantic Movement

Near the end of the eighteenth century, Europe began to be swept by a new movement in literature and the arts known as romanticism—a revolt against the artificial elements of eighteenth-century society, the cult of classicism and of the Age of Reason. In France this movement, which had its beginnings in the period of the French Revolution, came to prominence during the Napoleonic era and lasted until approximately the middle of the nineteenth century. It made itself felt in painting, in music, and especially in literature. French romanticism did not, however, attain its full development until the second decade of the nineteenth century.

The French romanticists protested against the traditional literary rules of classicism. They demanded that reason in literature should be replaced by imagination and emotion and that an author should be free to expose the innermost secrets of his heart. They exalted the individual, particularly one who had revolted against an oppressor. They revelled in striking contrasts and in violent human passions, frequently launched into divergent and eloquent discussions, and developed theories concerning their subject matter. They were often highly emotional, and sentimentality commonly played an important role in their works. They put particular emphasis on one outstanding feature of their writings: they concentrated on being especially careful to portray faithfully and in every detail the country and the period about which they wrote. This aspect of romanticism in France was called *cultiver la couleur locale* ("to cultivate local color").

Mérimée too, in his early literary endeavors, tried zealously to cultivate that local color so ardently advocated in romantic theory. It must be borne in mind that the struggle for supremacy was still being waged between the two literary schools—the classicists and the romanticists—when he began his literary career in the mid-1820s. Looking back to those early years as an author, Mérimée later recalled the superlative importance of local color at that time. As he wrote in his 1840 preface to *La Guzla:*

> In the Year of our Lord 1827 I was a *romantic.* We used to say to the *classics:* "Your Greeks are not at all Greeks, your Romans are not at all Romans; you do not know how to give your compositions *local color.* No salvation without *local color.*" We understood by *local color* what in the seventeenth century one called *moeurs:* but we were very proud of our word, and we thought we had imagined the word and the thing. In the matter of poems, we admired only the foreign and the most ancient; the ballads of the Scottish frontier, the romances of the Cid, these appeared to us to be incomparable masterpieces, always because of *local color.*

The leading literary figures of French romanticism were Victor Hugo (1802-1885), Alphonse de Lamartine (1790-1869), Alfred de Vigny (1797-1863), Alfred de Musset (1810-1857), Alexandre Dumas, père, (1803-1870), Marie-Henri Beyle (1783-1842), who wrote under the name Stendhal, and Prosper Mérimée (1803-1870). To a certain extent two earlier writers, François René de Chateaubriand (1768-1848) and Anne Louise Germaine Necker de Staël-Holstein (1766-1817), better known simply as Madame de Staël, also participated in the romantic movement in France.

Of the writers listed above, the man whose works were thoroughly romantic and largely neglected in his own lifetime but came into prominence only after his death was Stendhal. Stendhal wrote both novels and literary criticism. In his novels the reader has the illusion of seeing the action from far off, as if it were taking place on a stage. Stendhal had the faculty of bringing his readers close to the action and into the hearts and minds of his characters, by setting down their innermost thoughts clearly and coldly. In his critical work, *Racine and Shakespeare* (1822), he proclaimed the superiority of the English over the French classic dramatists. His novels *The Red and the Black* and *The Charterhouse of Parma* are now among the most famous novels in French literature and have gained an honored place among the great literary works of the world.

In addition to the authors noted above, three famous French writers began as staunch supporters of romanticism in their early works but later turned their backs on this movement; as we shall show later, the same thing is at least partially true of Prosper Mérimée. The first of the three, Charles Augustin Sainte-Beuve (1804-1869) was in his youth decidedly romantic in his leaning, but in later life he became a conservative critic—one of the greatest—who in his *Monday Chats* and *New Monday Chats* maintained that in classic as well as in romantic literature there is much that is of the highest order. The second of the three writers in question is Théophile Gautier (1811-1872), also an ardent supporter of romanticism in his youth, who in later life wrote poetry which was very definitely not romantic, particularly the flawless and impersonal lyrics in his *Enamels and Cameos*, his masterpiece. The third writer is probably the best-known woman in French literature, Lucile-Aurore Dupin (1804-1876)—known universally by her pen name George Sand. Her earlier novels—*Valentine, Lélia,* and *Jacques*—are decidedly romantic, but her later works—*The Devil's Pool* and *Little Fadette*—show a calmer, more realistic spirit. On the other hand, the great French novelist Honoré de Balzac (1799-1850), who lived through the entire romantic era, was affected little by the literary currents of his time.

By the year 1850, romanticism had run its course in France as elsewhere in Europe. A new spirit was in the air, a scientific spirit which demanded careful observation and suppressed emotion. The era of realism (Gustave Flaubert, 1821-1880, and Guy de Maupassant, 1850-1893) and later of naturalism (Émile Zola, 1840-1902) was at hand.

The question which now comes to mind is this: What was Mérimée's attitude toward romanticism? In the 1840s when he wrote *Colomba* (1840) and *Carmen* (1845), he had greatly changed his opinion regarding the imperative local color theory of the French romanticists, to which we have referred earlier. On the very first page of his *Colomba,* in fact, he stated clearly that the words *local color* in 1840 appeared to him to be a dead formula. With this rejection of local color he actually renounced romanticism as a movement.

There was, in fact, a reason for his change of view, a reason that coincided with his personality. In the 1820s and 1830s Victor Hugo assumed the direction of the romantic movement in France. This literary revolution, which had been so staunchly prepared and advocated by Mérimée and his fellow authors—who were almost exclusively aristocrats—before the advent of Victor Hugo, was now publicized with rather gaudy ostentatation in order to gain the applause of the general public. Precisely at that moment Mérimée lost interest in the struggle. As long as romanticism was the new literary movement advocated and zealously fostered by a few select and superior intellects, he made it his own cause; however, as soon as it became the property of the public at large, he was no longer interested. Moreover, his essentially aristocratic and conservative character rejected the passion and the enthusiasm which the young authors of the movement now put into their works. Their style and treatment of their subject matter was diametrically opposed to his own style and treatment of his material. He continued to write on romantic subjects, but he treated them in his own individual manner, namely, with a reserve and an irony which was effective, even though it was at times rather forced.

It is, indeed, difficult to class Prosper Mérimée as belonging completely to any one literary school. It is conceded by all that he is not a classicist in the French sense of the term, for he does not transfer human passion into an ideal world or an unreal world; he remains earthbound and human. Agreement comes to an end here, however, for some regard him as a romanticist, while others look upon him as a realist. Actually, Mérimée, the man and the writer, is a little of both: the subjects he chooses stamp him as a romanticist; his clear, cold, and completely impersonal style make his treatment of his chosen subject-matter that of a realist. Indeed, it was this highly conservative, restrained, and objective style which was held in such high regard by many of his contemporaries as the source of his power and originality. This was true to such a degree that it caused some of them to hail him as *l'artiste parfait* ("the perfect artist").

Mérimée's Personality and its Effect on his Work

Under the tutelage of Stendhal, Mérimée became a skeptic who, as Hippolyte Taine pointed out, "through fear of being duped in life, in love, in science, in art," harbored a distrust not only of himself, but also of society in general. In his literary endeavors this skepticism or distrust is revealed by a rigorous self-criticism, which inhibited his imagination. In Mérimée's historical works this meant absolute certainty of the statements he made, disciplined suppression of suggestion and imagination, and an interpretation which is both objective to the highest degree and as cold as ice. Moreover, he perfected his critical faculty to such a high degree that his works of criticism were crystal clear, concise, and controlled. So much was this the case that before Mérimée was thirty years old, Goethe had already compared his works and the personalities presented in them to "those perfect watches, in transparent crystal, on which can be seen at the same time the exact hour and all the play of the interior mechanism."

It was Stendhal who left to posterity the following portrait of him, which is not only analytically accurate but also clearly true:

> Prosper Mérimée was a young man in a gray frock-coat, very ugly, and with a turned-up nose. This young man had something insolent and extremely unpleasant about him. His eyes, small and without expression, had always the same look, and this look was ill-natured. Such was my first

impression of the best of my present friends. I am not
completely sure of his heart, but I am sure of his talents. A
letter from Count Gazul—now so well known—came to me
last week and made me happy for two days. His mother has a
great deal of French wit and a superior intelligence. It seems
to me that she, like her son, might give way to emotion once a
year.

Mérimée's personality was really a strange jumble of
contradictions. Apparantly he tried to disguise his true nature as
much as possible. He wanted to be regarded as cynical, cold,
suspicious, and selfish. In spite of this veneer, he spent a portion
of his salary as a senator on a pension for an unfortunate man who
had fallen into financial ruin due to the vicissitudes of politics,
made a supreme effort to sell Stendhal's manuscripts in order
to help the latter's destitute sister, and launched a new edition of
the naturalist Jacquemant's works in order to get money for the
latter's needy nephew. He pretended to have no faith in human
affections, yet he was a model son and formed throughout his life
a multitude of warm, human friendships. Posing all his life as a
cosmopolitan citizen of the world, he disdained nationalism and
patriotism with scorn and sarcasm, yet he collapsed when he
heard of the defeat of France at Wissembourg in 1870 during the
Franco-Prussian War. He regarded women as fickle and wicked
creatures belonging to the same genus as the cat and the tiger,
yet he voluntarily confided his innermost thoughts to Jenny
Dacquin (his "Unknown Lady"), to the Countess of Montijo, and
to the Empress Eugénie, without considering that they too might
prove false. His religious views were deistic and skeptical, yet his
last will and testament prescribed that he be buried by a pastor of
the Augsburg Confession.

Mérimée differs from other romanticists by not launching
into eloquent discussions and by not developing a theory
concerning his subject; he also allows the facts to speak for
themselves, offering no opinion and no judgment on either the
thoughts or the actions of his characters. Fearing constantly that
he might lose his self-control and betray his feelings, he evokes

emotions which stem not from his style but rather from the
events themselves, which he presents in his tales.

Mérimée's Attitude Toward Women

Though Mérimée's dominant quality in real life was his reserve,
in his novels and novellas his sympathy would often seem to be
bestowed upon bandits, criminals, and hot-tempered, violent
characters. He also liked to depict perverse and cruel women. All
these types he treats in a manner which shows his marked
preference for romantic subjects. In *The Opportunity* (*L'Occasion*) a fourteen-year-old girl takes poison and then kills her rival
in the same manner because both have had an unlawful passion
for a priest; in *Mateo Falcone*, the father decides to kill his little
son in cold blood by shooting him; in *Colomba*, the heroine, the
incarnation of unwholesome prejudice and hatred, wreaks a
fearful vengeance on her enemies; in *Carmen*, the fatal passion
of Don José for the diabolical gypsy girl, Carmen, bursts forth in
all its fury and tragedy; in *Lokis*, a young man is presented whose
ferocious instincts drive him to tear to pieces with his teeth the
girl whom he had vowed to love forever when he married her. In
reality, however, all of these subjects are treated by Mérimée
with supreme indifference. He is the scholar who handles his
themes with the greatest possible objectivity in a style which is
completely cold and unmoved by any emotion. In short, his tales
are presented to his readers in the same highly restrained,
matter-of-fact way as are his historical works.

The female characters in many of Mérimée's tales are
depicted as—among other things—frivolous, fickle, evil, crimi-
nal, perverse, and cruel. Mérimée never married, but curiously
enough he did enjoy the friendship of a considerable number of
women. The most famous of these friendships, except the
beginnings of a romance with George Sand (the *femme fatale* for
both Alfred de Musset and Frédéric Chopin), were his relations

with his "Unknown Lady" (*L'Inconnue*), with whom he even-
tually became acquainted; with the Countess of Montijo, whom
he met in Madrid in 1830; and with the Countess of Montijo's
daughter, Eugénie, who later became the Empress Eugénie,
wife of Napoleon III. The lady with whom he carried on a
correspondence for many years in his *Letters to Another
Unknown Lady*, which were published after Mérimée's death,
never identified herself.

After his *Chronicle of the Reign of Charles IX*, was
published, Mérimée received a letter (in 1831) which was
intelligent and interesting and which he deemed to be worthy of a
reply. This letter purported to be from an English lady of high
rank, who at the time remained anonymous. He did actually reply
and the correspondence thus initiated was continued between
the author and his *inconnue* for nine years. In 1840 Mérimée
finally learned who his "unknown lady" really was. He met her
in London and discovered that she was not an English
noblewoman at all, but rather the daughter of a French notary
from Boulogne-sur-Mer. Her name was Jenny Dacquin. Later
she lived in Paris in order to be closer to Mérimée, but even
though they were apparently in love, they did not marry. After
the author's death, Mlle. Dacquin revealed her correspondence
with Mérimée by publishing it under the title *Letters to an
Unknown Lady* (*Lettres à une inconnue*). Jenny Dacquin must
therefore not be confused with the second "unknown lady" in
Mérimée's life, who has never revealed her identity.

In 1830 Mérimée met the Countess of Montijo in Madrid,
while traveling in Spain. She too came to live in Paris later witn
her family, and Mérimée was a welcome and a frequent visitor in
her home. It was here that he became the particular favorite of
the Countess' daughter Eugénie. Later as Napoleon III's
Empress, Eugénie did not forget her old friend Mérimée.
Through her influence he was made a senator of the empire and
in this capacity he was often called upon to give his opinion and
counsel in delicate matters of great political importance. In
return for his excellent services, he was decorated by Napoleon

himself in 1866 with the Cross of Grand Officer of the Legion of Honor.

A share in Mérimée's work belonged to Eugénie's mother, the Countess of Montijo. She was chiefly responsible for one of his most celebrated tales, for it was she who told him in detail the story of *Carmen*, published in 1845. She also urged him to write his *History of Don Pedro I, King of Castile*. The Countess felt that the reputation of this Don Pedro, who was nicknamed "The Cruel," was unjust; she was able to persuade Mérimée that this rather notorious king had been maliciously slandered. Mérimée thus found himself saddled with the task of proving that Don Pedro may have been a so-called tyrant, but because he had only the interest of his subjects at heart, he must be regarded not as a "cruel, unjust tyrant" but rather as a "good, benevolent tyrant." Sharing the Countess' view, Mérimée argued that genuine democracy is merely an illusion, and that a "good tyrant" is necessary to make his people happy. To give Don Pedro the Cruel the appearance of such an ideal monarch, however, was nearly an impossible task, even for Prosper Mérimée.

In Mérimée's *Letters to Another Unknown Lady* (*Lettres à une autre inconnue*), we find him progressing slowly from coldness to skepticism to a genuine love affair, which buoyed him and agitated him for over thirty years. According to Arthur Symons, Mérimée apparently regarded this woman, who succeeded in remaining anonymous, as the embodiment of a type for which he had always shown a preference: the vivacious and seductive but unscrupulous and corrupt female "with wicked eyes." Such is Mariquita in Mérimée's *Clara Gazul's Theatre* (1825), who bedazzles the Grand Inquisitor "with her big black eyes, like the eyes of a young cat, soft and wicked at the same time." Such too is Carmen, the incarnation of wickedness, seduction, and infidelity, whose "big black eyes" haunt and lure Don José the bandit back to her again and again. Likewise, such is the girl he found near the end of his life in a novel by Turgenev. Mérimée showed a preference for this work because the heroine is "one of those diabolical creatures whose coquetry is the more dangerous because it is capable of passion."

Carmen as Literature and Opera

In the 1840s Mérimée became more and more interested in Russian literature. He learned the Russian language and studied the Russians, but somehow he never really discovered the mystery of the Russian soul. Once, however, when referring to the tales of Pushkin, who was a special favorite of his, his words were exactly on target. He called these tales "magnificent things, things after my own heart—that is to say, Greek in their truth and in their simplicity." What Mérimée has written here regarding Pushkin's tales might be applied with equal truth to the best of his own stories. The latter present elemental passions as hard, brutal facts and are detached, as it were, from their own sentiments. Indeed, if it were not for Mérimée's superb mastery of his material and his technique as a storyteller, his tales might easily have been melodramatic.

Such a tale is his *Carmen*. Taken out of Mérimée's hands, it was converted into a somewhat melodramatic libretto by Henri Meilhac and Ludovic Halévy, and has become one of the most popular of modern operas. Prosper Mérimée genuinely loved Spain. The bits of authentic local color added by the author and the philological discussion of the Romany language and the Calli are not only interesting, but also highly significant. Commenting on Mérimée's *Carmen*, Arthur Symons claims that "in this story all the qualities of Mérimée come into agreement; the student of human passions, the traveller, the observer, the learned man meet in harmony; and, in addition, there is the *aficionado*, the true *amateur*, in love with Spain and the Spaniards."

Mérimée's story of Carmen and Don José is a superb example of his art as a storyteller. It is colorful, romantic, very Spanish, well-knit, and gripping from beginning to end. The author's knowledge of the gypsies, their customs, their way of life, and their language has the ring of truth. In a word, Mérimée's *Carmen* is an excellent work of literature in its own right. What has made it even more popular and universally loved, however, is Georges Bizet's delightful and world-famous opera of the same name. Mérimée's tale, dramatized by the well-known librettists Henri Meilhac and Ludovic Halévy and set to Bizet's superb music, sent Friedrich Nietzsche into raptures of praise. It was first presented to the world at the National Opéra-Comique in Paris on March 3, 1875.

The libretto, although somewhat changed and greatly abbreviated, follows the various episodes of the love story as found in Mérimée's tale. Nevertheless, it does present some differences. In the first place, the French archeologist and geographer who reports the story in Mérimée's work has been omitted altogether. The technique of having the tragedy told in retrospect by the imprisoned Don José to the Frenchman, who is the narrator, has also been changed; their love story is presented directly on the stage in Bizet's opera. The framework—the story-within-a-story in Mérimée's original—has thus been eliminated by Meilhac and Halévy in their libretto, and the love story without embellishment constitutes the opera.

In the libretto, moreover, certain characters have been added with given names which are not found in Mérimée: *Zúñiga*, a captain; *Morales*, a brigadier; *Frasquita* and *Mercedes*, gypsy friends of Carmen; and particularly *Micaela*, a peasant girl, Don José's childhood sweetheart in his native Navarrese village, who brings him tidings of his ill and later dying mother. Certain characters and names in Mérimée—*Longo, Mina, Chapalangarra*—have been omitted in the libretto. The *picador* named *Lucas* in Mérimée's original has become a *toreador* named *Escamillo* in the opera. Other characters and names are the same in both. In the libretto, Carmen's death takes place outside the Plaza de Toros, or bullfighting arena, in Seville, while the cheers of the crowd are heard acclaiming Escamillo's victory, but in Mérimée's account she dies in the open country far from the city and from the *picador*

Lucas, her new lover. Omitted in the opera is Don José's suggestion to Carmen that she accompany him to the New World in order to start life anew, as is the scene between Don José and the priest immediately before the bandit stabs Carmen to death. As might be expected, Mérimée's dissertation in the final section of his story on gypsies generally—their life, manners, and customs, and their Romany language—is not included in the libretto of Bizet's opera.

In addition to the major differences noted above, there are other minor ones as well. Rather than enumerate these insignificant variants, we turn now to Bizet's opera and a brief summary of the plot of Meilhac and Halévy's libretto. This is followed by our modern English translation of Mérimée's story *Carmen*.

Georges Bizet's Opera *Carmen*

The Scene and Plot of Each of the Four Acts
(Meilhac and Halévy's Libretto)

The scene of the opera is Seville and its environs, the time, 1820.

Act I	A public square in Seville
Act II	Lillas Pastia's tavern in the suburbs of Seville
Act III	A wild mountain pass
Act IV	A public square at the entrance to the Plaza de Toros in Seville

ACT I

The opening scene of Act I is a public square in Seville, gay with an animated throng of people. In the foreground the military guards are stationed in front of their quarters. The cigarette factory is located to the right, and a bridge across the river is shown in the background. Morales, officer of dragoons, is lounging with the soldiers of the guard in front of the guardhouse, watching the people come and go. Among them he notices Micaela, a young peasant girl, who has come to look for Don José, whom she has loved since childhood. She bears a message for him from his mother. Her shy glances are searching for a familiar face among the soldiers. Morales questions her, and she tells him that she must see Don José, a corporal in the regiment. She then evades the too-pressing attentions of the soldiers, declines their invitation to remain, and hastily leaves the square. The relief guard, with Don José and his captain, Zúñiga, appears, and the other guard marches off.

At the stroke of noon, the cigarette girls appear, streaming out from the adjacent tobacco factory. Last of all comes Carmen, the beautiful, bold, heartless gypsy girl, their leading spirit in love and adventure, who is as reckless as she is bewitching. Scoffing at the pressing throng of gallants and suitors who crowd around her to gain her favor, she sings in reply the gay *Habanera*. The men invite her to choose a new lover among them, and her eye chances to light upon Don José, who up to then had been quite oblivious of her presence. The handsome young corporal takes her fancy. After a momentary hesitation she approaches him, tosses a flower in his face, and, with a passionate glance, laughingly flees, leaving Don José dazed and bewildered by her beauty and by the fascinating flash of her black eyes.

Against his will, Don José is flattered by such a token of partiality on the part of Carmen. He is presently surprised by his village sweetheart, Micaela. From his mother she brings him a message which exhorts him to be true to his first love, and with it she brings a kiss. The purity and innocence of Micaela is here presented as a foil to the worldliness and the riper attractions of Carmen. Micaela discreetly withdraws after a tender farewell, while Don José reads the letter from his mother. Filled with tender thoughts of earlier and happier days and memories of his old home, he is on the point of renouncing the fleeting passion inspired by Carmen.

While he is musing thus, a sudden commotion within the cigarette factory breaks in upon this softer mood. A stabbing fracas, in which Carmen has wounded a rival factory girl, leads to the gypsy's arrest, and Don José himself is ordered by Zúñiga to guard her and take her off to jail. Her passionate wiles, her smiles, and her softly spoken words outweigh and overpower his resolutions. Carmen's powers of fascination melt Don José's resistance and, after singing the provocative *Seguidilla*, she easily persuades him to let her escape. There is a sudden struggle and confusion. Don José releases his hold on Carmen, and she escapes, promising to meet him at the den of Lillas Pastia just outside the ramparts of Seville. The corporal is punished by imprisonment.

ACT II

Act II takes place in suburban Seville in the bohemian tavern of Lillas Pastia, a resort of smugglers, gypsies, and unsavory characters. Carmen is their faithful ally; she sings a wild gypsy tune depicting the gaiety and the reckless abandon which reigns here. She is here now to keep her promise to meet Don José and thinks of him, the man who went to prison for her sake. She passes the time pleasantly in the company of Zúñiga and other officers. Her musings are interrupted by the arrival of a procession in honor of Escamillo, a famous and popular *toreador*, whose appearance is followed by the well-known *Toreador Song*. Escamillo falls in love with Carmen. She, however, repulses his advances, and Escamillo leaves.

Meanwhile, two gypsies, Dancairo and Remendado, leaders of the smugglers, have entered the inn. They inform Carmen and her two companions, Frasquita and Mercedes, that there is a smuggling expedition afoot and that their aid is needed this same evening to pass some "merchandise." They ask Carmen to accompany them, but she is waiting to meet Don José, who has just been set free. She refuses to go until she has seen him. Presently Don José's voice is heard in the distance and he arrives. The rest retire, leaving him alone with Carmen, and there is an ardent love scene between the two.

Enchanted at recovering her admirer, Carmen performs her wild gypsy dance for him and employs all her wiles to entertain and fascinate the stolid soldier in order to induce him to join the band of smugglers. But her efforts are in vain, for in the midst of this reunion suddenly Don José hears distant regimental bugles sounding the retreat. He realizes that he will be treated as a deserter if he is found to be absent without leave from his quarters. In spite of Carmen's pleading, astonishment, and growing disdain and rage, he knows he must leave her. Carmen is furious, sings the sarcastic song *To Your Quarters?*, and flings his cap and sabre at him, bidding him begone. Desperate at the thought of losing her forever, Don José shows Carmen the flower which she tossed at him at their first meeting. He had cherished and preserved this flower; he sings the lovely *Flower Song*. Carmen then paints in glowing colors the joys of gypsy life which might be his, if he would only desert his regiment and follow her. But duty triumphs and Don José prepares to depart.

He is in the very act of leaving, when the door is forced open by the overbearing Zúñiga, his captain. Peremptorily he orders Don José to return at once to his quarters, but the latter just as haughtily refuses to yield to his rival and defies his army superior. Swords are drawn, but Carmen intervenes and summons the gypsies from their hiding-places. Zúñiga is overpowered, disarmed, and bound by the smugglers. Don José is forced, as an open mutineer against his superior officer, to desert his regiment, leave Seville, and join the smugglers. He departs with them on their expedition as Act II comes to an end.

ACT III

Act III opens as the smugglers are entering their rocky lair in a wild mountain gorge. They are pictured preparing their camp for the night, awaiting the coming of the dawn in order to carry their goods into the city. Don José is also there, but it is evident that he is already repenting his folly. He takes no interest in the enterprise at hand, for the career of a bandit is one to which a soldier does not easily succumb. Bitter regrets continually assail him; this obvious distaste on his part offends Carmen who, already tiring of her half-hearted lover, tauntingly bids him to go back home to his mother. He then joins Frasquita and Mercedes, who are telling fortunes with cards. The cards, in which she believes implicitly in true gypsy fashion, foretell that she is doomed to the speedy death which Don José's gloomy looks presage. Nonetheless she continues to tease him.

The robber band departs, leaving Don José to stand guard over the remainder of the goods. In this strained situation, two visitors arrive. The first is Don José's country sweetheart, Micaela. In his fascination for the wayward Carmen, Don José has forgotten Micaela, who really loves him. She catches sight of him, but at the same instant he levels his carbine and fires in her direction. Overcome by fright, Micaela swoons and sinks down behind the rocks.

The shot, however, was aimed at a second arrival, a stranger to Don José, who proved to be Escamillo, *toreador* of Granada. He clambers unharmed over the rocks, and introduces himself to Don José, who takes great pleasure in their meeting. This pleasure, however, quickly turns to hatred when, comparing notes, Escamillo nonchalantly announces his errand—to meet *his* sweetheart, Carmen. When Don José learns that they are rivals for Carmen, he challenges Escamillo to a duel. They fight with the deadly *navajas* (large, keen-bladed clasp-knives). Escamillo's life is saved by the unexpected and timely intervention of Carmen herself, whose love is now wholly transferred to him. Don José cannot resist Carmen's appeal and defiantly prepares to leave the scene. His decision to leave is interrupted by the appearance of Micaela. She has awakened from her swoon and implores Don José to hasten to his dying mother. Scornfully, Carmen echoes Micaela's request. To leave his rival Escamillo in sole possession of the field is too much for Don José; he swears never to be parted from Carmen until death. Nevertheless, he cannot resist Micaela's appeal. He finally departs, but he warns Carmen that they will meet again elsewhere and vows that he then will have his revenge.

The *Toreador Chorus* at the end of this act symbolizes the triumph of Escamillo in Carmen's affection and is an omen.

ACT IV

The scene of Act IV is a square in Seville, in front of the Plaza de Toros—the ancient amphitheatre in which the bullfights are held. This arena is the scene of Escamillo's triumphs in the bull ring. Following the brilliant procession, formed by the participants in the combat which is about to begin, come Escamillo and Carmen. She is radiant with delight in her latest conquest. An animated crowd awaits the procession. Orange sellers, hawkers of fans, and ice cream vendors press their wares on the waiting crowd in an atmosphere which is very gay. Carmen has returned to Seville to witness the triumph of her new-found love, Escamillo. He promises to fight the better because of his loved one's presence, and Carmen, with a premonition of what is to come, vows that she is willing to die for him.

Carmen's friends warn her to go away, telling her that Don José is lying in wait for her, half-crazed with jealousy and capable of desperate deeds. She does not heed their warning, however, replying that she has no fear of him. Soon thereafter the two meet, but Don José, though maddened, is not in a murderous mood. For the time being, love has gained mastery over his other feelings. With dramatic intensity he makes a last appeal to Carmen to return to him and be his, even promising to rejoin the band of smugglers for her sake. To each request made by Don José Carmen replies with a disdainful negative. She repels Don José with inflexible determination, laughs him to scorn, and after her final refusal she throws at his feet the ring he had given her. Although she knows that it may mean death, she continues fearlessly and recklessly to confront his rising fury. She tells him that all is over betweem them, that he means nothing at all to her, that Escamillo has replaced him and is now everything to her, and that she will love Escamillo to her last breath.

Exulting in the outburst of applause from the arena, which reveals Escamillo's victory, Carmen then attempts to join him. At this point, Don José, infuriated and madly jealous, seizes her and stabs her. Thus Carmen's death comes swiftly at the very moment when Escamillo, flushed with victory, comes from the arena, where the exultant throng is heard acclaiming his latest triumph in the bull ring.

The last notes of the opera are sung by the stricken Don José, who addresses a few pitiful words to the fallen form of his beloved Carmen, now silent in death.

A Brief Commentary on the Plot

The plot just sketched in outline is based on Prosper Mérimée's story, *Carmen*, a modern English translation of which is herewith presented. The very skillfully adapted libretto of the opera is the joint production of Henri Meilhac and Ludovic Halévy. The action is animated, well-knit, and flowing—it never drags or becomes tiresome. It was a master stroke indeed to introduce into the opera the character of Micaela (who is not found in Mérimée's tale) as a contrast and foil to that of Carmen. An opportunity for musical characterization was thus presented, and Bizet made it one of the most attractive and effective features in a work replete with charming and striking musical effects. Indeed, so splendid and beautiful were these effects that the great German philosopher Friedrich Nietzsche was ecstatic in his praise of Bizet's music in *Carmen.*

Georges Bizet was thoroughly acquainted with Spanish folkways and folk music owing to his frequent sojourns in the Pyrenees. Consequently, he portrayed scenes and personages in the magical light of real "local color." His melodies, however, except for the *Habanera,* were entirely his own.

The leading character, Carmen, occupies the foreground in Bizet's opera, dramatically and musically, whenever she is on the stage. Despite this, the lesser roles are so carefully handled that there is no sense of disproportion. As a result, the total effect is that of a great work of art, skillfully wrought.

Pertinent Facts in the Life of Georges Bizet and the Opera

Georges Bizet was a native of Paris, where he was born on October 25, 1838. He died there thirty-seven years later. Because of his unusual talent, he was accepted as a pupil at the Paris Conservatory at the tender age of nine. In 1857, before the age of twenty, he won the Prix de Rome; in the same year his first opera, *Docteur Miracle,* was produced. Other productions followed, among which *Les Pecheurs de Perles* (*The Pearl Fishers*), first presented to the public in 1863, deserves special mention. His

Carmen, the last and greatest opera composed by Bizet, was first performed at the Opéra-Comique in Paris on March 3, 1875.

Bizet was far too original in his compositions, however, to satisfy the Parisian audiences of his day. They supported neither his operas nor his orchestral works. When he presented *Carmen* to them in 1875, it was received with a storm of abuse. It was immoral; it was Wagnerian—and anything that resembled Wagner was at that time a deadly sin in France!

How wrong they were is shown by the fact that the supreme merits of *Carmen* have won for it a place among the two or three most often performed operas in modern repertory. Its music and its story are loved by all, appealing equally to trained musicians and to amateurs. Bizet's superb talents are shown by his remarkable lyric gifts. He is able to handle dramatic scenes with the freedom demanded by modern opera. In passing, it should be mentioned that one of the most popular sections of the opera *Carmen* was not written by Bizet: the *Habanera*—a stately Cuban dance. It was the work of Sebastian Yradier (1809-1869), a Spanish composer who lived part of his life in Cuba.

Bizet's heart was not strong, and it is possible that due to the hostile reception of *Carmen*, he died of grief in June, 1875—three months after its first performance in Paris. The music he wrote in his short life-time will long survive him, and chief among the works into which he ungrudgingly poured his life's energy was *Carmen*. No finer eulogy could be paid to any man than the one paid to Bizet by Friedrich Nietzsche, when he wrote: "I become a better man when this Bizet speaks to me in his music!"

To the Reader: Prosper Mérimée's *Carmen* contains a considerable number of words and phrases from the gypsy language known as Romany and also from the Basque tongue, as well as from Spanish. To translate them into English would cause this fine story to lose much of its local color, flavor, and verve. Some statements would even suffer to such a degree in translation as to become virtually meaningless unless the foreign word or words were retained.

Various local, geographical, literary, and historical terms and references in the text, which are specifically Spanish and are not commonly known, also require an explanation in order to make their full significance completely clear.

For these reasons, I have compiled a list of notes (each of which has been numbered to correspond to the number printed after the word or phrase in the text which need to be clarified). Readers are thus afforded an opportunity not only to understand the story better, but also to extend their general knowledge by referring to the notes, where these interesting terms and customs are explained. These annotations immediately follow the text on page 88.

CÉCILE THÉVENET
OPÉRA, PARIS

GERMAINE BAILAC
OPÉRA-COMIQUE

DELNA

DE NUOVINA

GALLI-MARIÉ
THE ORIGINAL CARMEN

DAVELLI
OPÉRA COMIQUE

MARIÉ DE L'ISLE

MÉRENTIÉ
OPÉRA, PARIS

ELENA SANZ

CHARLOTTE WYNS

BRESSLER-GIANOLI
OPÉRA COMIQUE

Some Famous Carmens of the Past

Πᾶσα γυνὴ χόλος ἐστίν· ἔχει δ'ἀγαθὰς δύο ὥρας
Τὴν μίαν ἐν θαλάμῳ, τὴν μίαν ἐν θανάτῳ. [1]
—Palladas.

Carmen – I

I have always suspected the geographers of not knowing what they are talking about when they place the battlefield of Munda in the Bastuli-Poeni country, near modern Monda, which is roughly five miles north of Marbella. According to my own conjectures, based on the text of the anonymous author of the *Bellum Hispaniense* [2] and some information gathered in the excellent library of the Duke of Ossuna, I thought it necessary to look in the neighborhood of Montilla for the memorable place where, for the last time, Caesar played double or nothing against the champions of the Republic. Finding myself in Andalusia in the early fall of 1830, I made a rather long excursion in order to clear up the doubts which still remained in my mind. A paper which I plan to publish soon will, I hope, leave no uncertainty in the minds of all bona-fide archaeologists. While waiting for my dissertation to solve at last this geographical riddle which is keeping the whole of learned Europe in suspense, I want to tell you a little story. It does not detract in any way from the interesting question of the location of Munda.

At Cordova I had hired a guide and two horses and started out for the country with Caesar's *Commentaries* and a few shirts as my entire baggage. One day, as I was wandering along the elevated portion of the Plain of Cachena dead tired, dying of thirst, and burned by a sun like molten lead, with all my heart I wished Caesar and the sons of Pompey to the devil. Then I noticed some distance from the path I was following a small, green patch of grass, dotted with rushes and reeds. This told me that a spring must be close by. In fact, as I approached I saw that the supposed grassy area was a swamp. Into this swamp there drained a brook which came, apparently, from a narrow gorge between two high foothills of the Sierra de Cabra. I concluded that if I were to go upstream, I would probably find fresh water, fewer leeches and frogs, and perhaps even a little shade among the rocks. At the entrance to the gorge my horse began to neigh, and another horse, which I could not see, immediately replied. I had walked scarcely a hundred paces when the gorge—suddenly widening—revealed a sort of natural amphitheatre, completely shaded by'the height of the steep slopes which surrounded it. It was impossible to come upon a spot which promised a more agreeable stopping-place for the traveller. At the foot of the steep rocks, the spring tumbled down bubbling and flowed into a little pool whose bottom was covered with sand as white as snow. Five or six beautiful holm oaks, always sheltered from the wind and refreshed by the spring, grew on its banks and covered it with their dense shade. Finally, around the pool a fine, glossy grass provided a better bed than was to be found in any inn for twenty-five miles round about.

The honor of discovering this fine spot did not belong to me. A man was already resting there and was no doubt asleep when I came along. Awakened by the whinnying, he had risen and gone back to his horse, which had, during his master's sleep, helped himself to a hearty meal of the grass all around him. He was a sturdy young fellow of medium height but stocky build, and his expression was stern and proud. His complexion, which originally might have been fair, had become even darker than his hair through the effect of the sun. In one hand he was holding the halter of his mount and in the other a brass musket. I admit that the musket and the fierce look of the man at first surprised me a bit, but because of hearing people talk about them and never meeting any, I no longer believed in robbers. Besides, I had seen so many honest farmers arm themselves to the teeth merely to go to market, that it seemed to me the sight of a gun did not give me the right to doubt the respectability of the stranger. "Anyhow," I said to myself, "what would he do with my shirts and my Elzevir edition of the *Commentaries?*"[3] So I greeted the man with the musket with a familiar nod of my head and, smiling, I asked him if I had disturbed his sleep. Without answering me, he sized me up from head to foot. Then, as if satisfied with his examination of me, he looked over my guide, who was coming up behind me, with the same attention. I saw the latter grow pale, stop, and show obvious terror on his face. "A nasty encounter," I said to myself, but prudence told me at once not to show any anxiety. I dismounted, instructed the guide to unbridle the horses and, kneeling at the edge of the spring, I plunged my head and my hands into the cool water. Then I drank a deep draught, lying flat on my stomach, as did the soldiers which Gideon spurned.[4]

At the same time, however, I was observing my guide and the stranger. The former was approaching very reluctantly, but the latter did not seem to have any evil designs against us, for he had now freed his horse, and his musket, which at first he held horizontally, was now aimed at the ground.

Believing that I ought not to take offense at the lack of concern he seemed to show at my coming, I stretched out on the grass and, in a very casual manner, asked this stranger with the gun whether he had a tinderbox on him. At the same time I pulled out my cigar case. The stranger, still without speaking, fumbled in his pocket, took out his tinderbox, and hastened to give me a light. Evidently he was becoming a little more human, for he sat down before me—not, however, without his musket. When my cigar was lit, I picked out the best one among those I had left and asked him if he smoked.

"Yes, sir," he replied.

These were the first words that he spoke, and I noticed that he did not pronounce the s in the Andalusian manner.[5] I concluded, therefore, that he was a traveller like myself, only less of an archaeologist.

"You'll find this one quite good," I told him, handing him a genuine Havana Royal.

With a slight bow of his head, he lit his cigar from mine, thanked me with another nod, and then began to smoke, apparently with very great pleasure.

"Ah!" he exclaimed, letting the smoke of his first puff slowly escape through his mouth and nostrils, "how long it's been since I've had a smoke!"

In Spain, a cigar given and accepted establishes relations of hospitality, as does the sharing of bread and salt in the Orient. The man before me now showed himself to be more talkative than I had expected him to be. Besides, even though he claimed to be a native of the district of Montilla, he did not seem to know the country well at all. He could not tell me the name of this charming valley where we happened to be, nor did he know the name of any village in the surrounding area. Finally, when I asked him if he had not seen close by the ruined walls some broad, flanged tiles and some sculptured stones, he confessed that he had never paid any attention to such things. On the other hand, he showed himself to be an expert on the subject of horses. He criticized mine, which was not difficult to do. Then he stated the pedigree of his own, which came from the famous stud farm of Cordova: a noble beast, in fact, so inured to fatigue—so his master claimed—that he had once covered seventy-five miles in a single day at a gallop or a fast trot. In the middle of his story the stranger then stopped suddenly as if he were surprised and annoyed at having said too much.

"The fact is that I was in a great hurry to get to Cordova," he continued with some embarrassment. "I had to see the judges about a trial. . . ." While he was speaking, he kept looking at my guide Antonio, who lowered his eyes.

The shade and the spring charmed me so much, that I remembered some slices of excellent ham which my friends in Montilla had packed in my guide's sack. I asked him to take them out and I invited the stranger to take his portion of the impromptu snack. If he hadn't smoked for a long time, it seemed to me that he probably had not eaten in the last forty-eight hours at least. He devoured the food like a famished wolf. I could not help thinking that our meeting had been providential for the poor devil. My guide, however, ate little, drank even less, and did not talk at all, even though from the beginning of our journey he had revealed himself to me as an unequalled chatterbox. The presence of our host seemed to worry him, and a certain distrust kept them aloof from one another without my being able to guess precisely the reason for it.

The last crumbs of bread and ham had already disappeared

and each of us had smoked a second cigar, when I ordered the guide to bridle our horses. I was just about to take leave of my new friend, when he asked me where I expected to spend the night.

Before I had paid any attention to a signal from my guide, I had answered that I was going to the Venta del Cuervo.

"A bad lodging for a person like yourself, sir, . . . I'm going there too and, if you'll permit me to accompany you, we'll travel together."

"Gladly," I said, mounting my horse.

My guide, who was holding my stirrups, gave me a new signal with his eyes. I answered him by shrugging my shoulders, as if to assure him that my mind was at ease, and we got under way.

Antonio's mysterious signals, his anxiety, some words which the stranger let fall, especially that seventy-five mile race of his and the implausible explanation that he had given concerning it, had already caused me to form my own opinion about my travelling companion. I had no doubt in my mind that I was dealing with a smuggler, perhaps even a bandit, but what did that matter to me? I knew the Spanish character well enough to be very sure that I had nothing to fear from a man who had eaten and smoked with me. His very presence was, in fact, a sure protection against every evil encounter. Besides, I was very glad to know what a bandit was really like. One does not see them every day, and there is a certain fascination in finding oneself near a dangerous person, especially when one feels that he is gentle and tractable.

By degrees I hoped to lead the stranger to confide in me and, in spite of my guide's winking, I turned the conversation to highwaymen. Naturally, I spoke about them with respect. In Andalusia there was at that time a famous bandit named José María, whose exploits were on the lips of all. "What if I were right here and now beside José María?" I said to myself. I then told the stories that I knew about this hero, all in his praise, morcovcr, and I loudly expressed my admiration for his bravery and generosity.

"José María is nothing but a rogue," said the stranger coldly.

"Is he doing himself justice, or is this excessive modesty on his part?" I wondered, for, simply by taking a close look at my companion, I had succeeded in applying to him the description of José María, which I had read posted on the gates of many a town in Andalusia. "Yes, he's the same one all right . . . ! Fair hair, blue eyes, wide mouth, fine teeth, small hands; an expensive shirt, a velvet jacket with silver buttons, white leather leggings, a bay horse . . . There's no doubt about it! But let's respect his incognito."

We arrived at the *venta*. It was just as he had described it to me, that is, one of the most wretched inns that I had ever seen. A large room served as the kitchen, the dining area, and the sleeping quarters. On a flat stone, the fire was already burning in the middle of the room; the smoke escaped through a hole cut in the roof or rather, it stopped and formed a cloud a few feet above the ground. Along the wall, five or six old mule blankets were to be seen stretched out on the floor. These were the travellers' beds. Twenty paces from the house, or rather, from the single room which I have just described, there rose a sort of shed that served as a stable. In this charming resort there were no other human beings, at least not at the moment, except an old woman and a little girl ten to twelve years of age, both the color of soot and clothed in horrible rags. "That's all that remains," I said to myself, "of the population of ancient Munda Baetica! O Caesar! O Sextus Pompeius! How shocked you'd be if you were to return to the world!"

Noticing my companion, the old woman uttered an exclamation of surprise.

"Ah! Don José!" she exclaimed.

Don José frowned and raised a hand with a gesture of authority which stopped the old woman at once. I turned toward my guide and by means of an unseen sign I made him understand that I knew what he was trying to tell me about the man with whom I was going to spend the night . . . .

The supper was better than I had expected. We were served on a little table one foot high an old rooster fricasseed with rice and many pimentos, then pimentos in oil, and finally some *gazpacho*, a kind of pimento salad. Three such strongly spiced dishes forced us to resort frequently to a goatskin of Montilla wine, which proved to be delicious. After we had eaten our meal, spying a mandolin hanging against the wall (in Spain there are mandolins everywhere), I asked the little girl who was serving us whether she knew how to play it.

"No," she replied, "but Don José plays it very well!"

"Please sing something for me," I said to him. "I am passionately fond of your national music."

"I can refuse nothing to such an honest gentleman who gives me such excellent cigars," exclaimed Don José with a good-humored look on his face.

Then, after the mandolin had been handed to him, he sang and accompanied himself on the instrument. His voice, although harsh, was pleasant, the tune melancholy and strange. As for the words, I didn't understand a single one.

"Unless I am mistaken," I said to him, "that's not a Spanish air that you've just sung. It sounds like the *zorzicos* that I've heard in the Basque provinces, and the words must be in the Basque tongue."[6]

"Yes," replied Don José in a sombre tone.

He set the mandolin down on the floor and, with arms folded, he began to gaze with a strange expression of sadness into the fire, which was going out. His face, lighted by a lamp which had been placed on the little table, was both noble and fierce, and reminded me of Milton's Satan. Perhaps, like him, my companion was thinking of the abode he had left for the exile which he had brought upon himself through transgression. I tried to revive the conversation, but he did not reply, absorbed as he was in his sad thoughts. The old woman was already lying down in a corner of the room, hidden by a blanket full of holes, which was stretched taut on a cord. The little girl had followed her into this retreat reserved for the fair sex. Rising, my guide then invited me to follow him to the stable, but at this sound of his voice, Don José, as though roused with a start, asked him in a brusque tone of voice where he was going.

"To the stable," replied the guide.

"What for? The horses have been fed. Lie down here; the gentleman will permit it."

"I fear that my master's horse may be sick. I should like my master to see him. Perhaps he will know what must be done for him."

It was obvious that Antonio wanted to talk to me privately, but I was eager not to make Don José suspicious. In the situation in which we found ourselves, it seemed to me that the best thing to do was to show the greatest confidence. I therefore answered Antonio that I knew nothing about horses, and that I felt like sleeping. Don José followed him to the stable, from which he returned alone a short time later. He told me that there was nothing wrong with the horse, but that my guide considered him to be so precious an animal that he was rubbing him down with his jacket in order to make him sweat, and that he expected to spend the night in this pleasant occupation. Meanwhile I had stretched out on the mule blankets, carefully wrapped up in my cloak in order not to touch them. After he had asked my pardon for the liberty which he was taking in settling down for the night near me, Don José lay down before the door, but not without first reloading his musket, which he was careful to put under the sack serving him as a pillow. Five minutes after we had said good night to each other, both of us were sound asleep.

I thought that I was tired enough to be able to sleep in such a lair, but in an hour's time some very unpleasant itching snatched me out of my first slumber. As soon as I understood the nature of this itching, I got up, convinced that it was better to spend the rest of the night outside under the stars than under this inhospitable roof. Walking on tiptoe, I reached the door by stepping over the bed of Don José, who was sleeping the sleep of the just; I did this so well that I was able to leave the house without waking him up. Next to the door was a wide wooden bench. I stretched out on it and settled down as best I could to sleep the rest of the night. I was going to close my eyes for the second time, when I seemed to see the shadows of a man and a horse passing in front of me, each walking without making even the slightest sound. I sat up, for I thought I recognized Antonio.

Surprised at seeing him out of the stable at such an hour, I got up and walked over to meet him. He had stopped, having seen me first.

"Where is he?" Antonio asked me in a whisper.

"He's sleeping in the *venta*. He's not afraid of the bedbugs. But why are you leading away this horse?"

I noticed then that Antonio had carefully wrapped the hoofs of the animal with the remains of an old blanket in order not to make any noise when leaving the shed.

"In Heaven's name, speak more softly," Antonio said to me. "Tell me, don't you know who that man is? He's José Navarro, the most notorious bandit in Andalusia. All day long I have been giving you signals which you've pretended not to understand."

"Bandit or not, what's that to me?" I replied. "He hasn't robbed us and I'd be willing to bet that he hasn't any intention of doing so."

"That's all very fine, but there are two hundred ducats for the man who turns him in. I know a lancer's station a league and a half from here, and before it's daylight I'll bring some husky fellows back here. I'd have taken his horse, but it's so mean that nobody but Navarro can get near it."

"May the devil take you!" I said to him. "What harm has this poor fellow done to you to denounce and report him? Besides, are you sure that he's the bandit you say he is?"

"Quite sure. A little while ago he followed me into the stable and said to me: 'You seem to recognize me. If you tell that good master of yours who I am, I'll blow your brains out.' Stay, sir, stay with him, you have nothing to fear. As long as he knows you're here, he won't suspect anything."

All the while that we were talking, we had already strayed quite far from the inn, so that the sound of the horse's shoes might not be heard. In a trice Antonio had rid the animal of the rags in which he had wrapped its hoofs. He was already straddling his mount. I tried begging and threats to restrain him.

"I'm a poor devil, sir," he said to me. "I can't afford to lose two hundred ducats, especially when it's a matter of freeing the land of such vermin. But take care! If Navarro wakes up, he'll leap to his musket and you beware! As for me, I've gone too far to turn back now. Manage as best you can!''

The rogue was in the saddle. He spurred his horse on both sides, and in the darkness I had soon lost sight of him.

I was very annoyed with my guide and also considerably worried. After a moment's reflexion, I came to a decision and returned to the inn. Don José was still sound asleep. He was undoubtedly restoring his vigor by sleeping away at this time the weariness and the vigils of many adventurous days. I was obliged to shake him violently in order to rouse him. Never will I forget his fierce look and the movement he made to grasp his musket which, as a precautionary measure, I had placed some distance from his bed.

"Sir," I said to him, "I beg your pardon for waking you, but I have a foolish question to ask you: Would you be very pleased to see a half dozen lancers come here?"

He leaped to his feet and shouted in a terrible voice:

"Who told you that?'' he asked me.

"It matters little where the information comes from, provided that it's correct.''

"Your guide has betrayed me, but he'll pay for it! Where is he?''

"I don't know . . . In the stable, I think . . . but someone has told me. . . .''

"Who told you? . . . It can't be the old woman. . . .''

"Someone I don't know. Without any further words: yes or no, do you have any reason not to wait for the soldiers? If you have, lose no time; if not, good night and I beg your pardon for having interrupted your sleep.''

"Ah! Your guide! Your guide! I mistrusted him from the very beginning . . . but . . . I'll settle my account with him! . . . Farewell, sir. May God reward you for the favor I owe you. I'm not altogether as bad as you think I am . . . Yes, there's still something in me which deserves the pity of a man of honor . . . Farewell, sir . . . I've only one regret, namely that I'm not able to pay my debt to you!''

"As a reward for the service I've shown you, promise me, Don José, not to suspect anyone, not to think of vengeance.

Come, here are some cigars for you on the road. Have a good journey!"

And I held out my hand to him.

He squeezed it without replying, took his musket and his sack and, after having spoken a few words to the old woman in a jargon I could not understand, he ran to the shed. A few moments later I heard him galloping away into the countryside.

As for me, I lay down again on my bench, but I did not go back to sleep a wink. I wondered whether I had done the right thing in saving a bandit, perhaps even a murderer, from the gallows, simply because I had eaten some ham with him and some rice cooked in the Valencian style. Had I not actually betrayed my guide, who was upholding the cause of justice? Had I not exposed him to the vengeance of a scoundrel? But what about the obligations of hospitality! ... A primitive prejudice, I told myself; now I shall have to answer for all the crimes the bandit is going to commit ... But is it really a prejudice, this subconscious instinct which resists all reasoning? Perhaps in the delicate situation in which I found myself, I could not extricate myself without remorse.

I was still wavering in the greatest uncertainty regarding the moral justification for my action, when I saw a half dozen horsemen appear with Antonio, who was staying prudently in the rear guard. I walked over to them and notified them that the bandit had fled more than two hours before. Questioned by the sergeant, the old woman answered that she knew Navarro but that, living alone, she would never have dared to risk her life by denouncing him. She added that whenever he came to her place, it was his habit always to leave in the middle of the night. As for me, I had to go with them some leagues away in order to show my passport and sign a declaration before a judge, after which I was allowed to go back again to my archaeological research.

Antonio held a grudge against me, because he suspected that I was the one who had prevented him from earning the two hundred ducats. However, we parted amically at Cordova, where I gave him as large a tip as the state of my finances would allow me to give.

Carmen – II

I spent some days in Cordova. I had been told about a certain manuscript in the library of the Dominican monastery in which I might find some interesting information about ancient Munda. I was very well received by the good fathers and spent my days in their monastery and my evenings strolling through the city. In Cordova toward sunset a number of idlers may be found on the embankment that runs along the right bank of the Guadalquivir river. There one breathes in the odors from a tannery which still maintains the old reputation of this region for the preparation of fine leather; but as a compensation one can enjoy a spectacle which definitely has its own merits. A few minutes before the Angelus, a large number of women gather at the edge of the river below the embankment, which is quite high. No man would dare to mix with this group. As soon as the Angelus rings out, it is considered to be night. At the last stroke of the bell, all these women undress and go into the water. Then there may be heard shouting, laughing, an infernal din. From the top of the embankment the men watch the bathers, opening their eyes wide, but not seeing very much. However, the white and vague forms which are outlined against the dark blue of the river cause their spirits to wax poetic, and with a little imagination it is not very difficult to see them as Diana and her nymphs at the bath, without having to fear the fate of Actaeon. [7]

People have told me that some wags pooled their money on a certain day to grease the palm of the cathedral bell ringer in order to have him ring out the Angelus twenty minutes before the lawful hour. Although it was still broad daylight, the nymphs of the Guadalquivir did not hesitate for a moment and, relying on the Angelus more than on the sun, with a clear conscience they took their bath, which is always very simple. I was not present. When I was there, the bell ringer was incorruptible and the dusk so black that only a cat could have distinguished the oldest orange peddler from the prettiest working girl in Cordova.

One evening at the hour when one can see nothing more, I was quietly smoking and leaning against the parapet of the embankment when a woman came up the stairway which leads to the river and sat down near me. In her hair she had a spray of jasmine, the petals of which diffuse an intoxicating perfume in the evening air. She was simply, indeed even poorly dressed, entirely in black, as are most of the working girls in the evening. Proper women wear black only in the morning; in the evening they dress *à la francesa*.

When she reached me, my bathing girl let the mantilla which covered her head slip down on her shoulders. In the dim starlight I saw that she was petite, young, and that she had a shapely figure and very big eyes. I threw away my cigar at once. She understood this highly French gesture of politeness, and hastened to tell me that she liked the smell of tobacco very much and that she herself even smoked when she found some very mild *papelitos*. Fortunately, I had some like that in my cigarette case, and I hastened to offer one to her. She deigned to take it and lit it from an end of a burning piece of rope which a child brought to us at the cost of a penny.

Blending the smoke of our two cigarettes, the bathing beauty and I chatted so long that the two of us found ourselves almost alone on the embankment. I thought that I was not being too forward when I offered to take her for some ice-cream at a nearby *nevería*.[8]   After first modestly hesitating, she accepted, but before making her decision she wanted to know what time it was. I made my watch chime, and this chiming seemed to astonish her very greatly.

"What inventions you have where you live, you foreign gentlemen! From what country do you come, sir? You are English,[9] no doubt?"

"French, and your humble servant. And you Miss, or Mrs., are from Cordova, I suppose?"

"No."

"Well, anyway, you're from Andalusia. I seem to recognize that from your soft speech."

"If you observe people's accent so well, you must be able to guess easily what I am."

"I think you are from the land of Jesus, on the very doorstep of Paradise. (I had learned this metaphor, which designates Andalusia, from my friend Francisco Sevilla, the well-known picador.)

"Paradise! Bah! . . . People from hereabouts say that it's not for us!"

"Well, then, you might be Moorish, or . . . . (I stopped short, not daring to say Jewish.)

"Come, come, now! You can see very well that I'm a gypsy. Do you want me to tell you *la baji?* [10] Have you ever heard of Carmencita, little Carmen? That's who I am."

I was such a frivolous person in those days, fifteen years ago, that I did not back away horrified at seeing myself next to a sorceress. "Fine," I said to myself. "Last week I shared my supper with a highwayman, today I'm going to eat ice cream with a handmaiden of the devil. When one travels, one must see everything."

But I had still another motive for cultivating her acquaintance. Now that I have finished school, I must confess, to my shame, that I had wasted some time studying the occult sciences. I had even tried several times to conjure up the prince of darkness. For a long time now I had been cured of my passion for such research; nevertheless, I still retained a certain curiosity about all superstitions, and I rejoiced to be able to find out to what extent the art of magic had developed among the gypsies.

Chatting during all this time, we had entered the *nevería*, where we sat down at a little table lighted by a candle enclosed in a glass globe. I thus had ample opportunity to examine my *gitana* at my leisure, while some respectable people, sitting there eating their ice cream, were amazed to see me in such fine company.

I doubt very much whether Carmen was a pure gypsy. At least she was infinitely prettier than all the women of her race I had ever met. "In order that a woman be pretty," say the Spaniards, "she must collect thirty affirmatives" or, if you will, people must be able to describe her affirmatively by means of ten adjectives, each one applicable to three parts of her person. For example, she must have three things black: eyes, eye-lashes, and eye-brows; three things thin: fingers, lips, hair, etc. Consult Brantôme for the rest.

My gypsy could lay no claim to so many perfections. Her skin, in addition to being perfectly smooth, was very nearly the color of copper. Her eyes were slanted, but beautifully shaped. Her lips were a bit heavy but well formed, and revealed teeth that were whiter than skinned almonds. Her hair, perhaps a little on the coarse side, was long, shiny, and black with a blue sheen like the wing of a raven. In order not to bore you with too wordy a description, I shall simply tell you that for each defect she possessed a quality which stood out perhaps more strongly by contrast. Hers was a strange, wild beauty, a face that at first was astonishing, but which was unforgettable. Her eyes especially had an expression both voluptuous and fierce, such as I have never found since in any human look. "A gypsy's eye is a wolf's eye," is a Spanish saying which shows accurate observation. If you have not the time to go to the zoo to study the expression of a wolf, look at your cat when he is ready to pounce on a sparrow.

I felt that it would have been ridiculous to have my fortune told in a cafe. I therefore asked the pretty sorceress to allow me to accompany her to her home. She readily agreed, but again she wanted to know what time it was and asked me once more to make my watch chime.

"Is it really gold?" she asked, looking at it with extraordinary attention.

When we again set out on our way, it was pitch dark. Most of the shops were closed and the streets were almost deserted. We crossed the bridge over the Guadalquivir, and at the far end of the outlying districts we stopped in front of a house which had in no wise a palatial appearance. A child opened the door for us. The gypsy girl said some words to him in a tongue that was unknown to me and which I have learned since to be *rommani* or *chipe calli*, the language of the *gitanos*. The child disappeared at once, leaving us alone in a rather large room, furnished with a little table, two stools, and a chest. I must not forget to mention a jug of water, a pile of oranges, and a string of onions.

As soon as we were alone, the gypsy girl took out of her coffer some cards which seemed to have been much used, a magnet, a desiccated chameleon, and some other objects necessary for her art. Then she told me to cross my left palm with a coin, and the magic ceremonies began. It is useless to report to you what her predictions were, and, as far as her technique was concerned, it was quite evident that she was no mean sorceress.

Unfortunately, we were soon interrupted. The door was suddenly opened violently and a man wrapped up to his eyes in a brown cloak entered the room, addressing the gypsy girl in a very rude manner. I did not understand what he was saying, but the tone of his voice indicated that he was in an extremely bad humor. On seeing him, the *gitana* exhibited neither surprise nor anger. She ran up to meet him, and with extraordinary volubility addressed a few sentences to him in the mysterious language which she had already used in my presence. The word *payllo*, foreigner, often repeated, was the only one that I understood. I knew that the gypsies designate by this word every man who is not of their race. Taking it for granted that my presence was in question, I was expecting a delicate situation. Already I had my hand on the leg of one of the stools, and I was debating with myself, trying to guess the exact moment when it would be right to throw it at the head of the intruder. The latter pushed the gypsy girl aside rudely and advanced toward me. Then, taking a step backward:

"Ah, sir," he said, "it's you!"

I looked at him in my turn and recognized my friend Don José. At this moment I regretted a little that I had not let him be hanged.

"Why, it's you, my fine fellow," I exclaimed laughing as naturally as I could. "You've interrupted the young lady just when she was telling me some very interesting things."

"Always the same! That must stop," he muttered between his teeth, casting a fierce look at her.

But the gypsy girl kept talking to him in her language. She was growing gradually more excited. Her eyes became bloodshot and terrified. Her features contracted and she stamped her foot. It seemed to me that she was urging him vehemently to do something about which he was displaying a certain hesitation. What it was I thought I understood only too well, by watching her pass her small hand rapidly back and forth under her chin. I was tempted to believe that it was a question of cutting someone's throat, and I had a certain suspicion that the throat in question was none other than mine.

During all this torrent of eloquence, Don José replied with only two or three words uttered in a curt tone of voice. The gypsy girl cast a look of profound scorn at him. Then, sitting down cross-legged in the Turkish style in a corner of the room, she selected an orange, peeled it, and began to eat it.

Don Jose took me by the arm, opened the door, and led me out into the street. We walked about two hundred paces in the most profound silence. Then, pointing with his hand, he said: "Keep on walking straight ahead and you'll find the bridge."

Immediately he turned his back upon me, and rapidly walked away. I returned to my inn a bit crestfallen and in quite a bad humor. The worst of it was that while undressing, I noticed that my watch was missing. Various considerations kept me from going to claim it the next day, or from requesting the *corregidor* to be so kind as to have it traced. I ended my work on the Dominicans' manuscript and left for Seville.

After several months of wandering about in Andalusia I wished to return to Madrid, and I had to pass through Cordova again. I had no intention of staying there long, for I had taken a dislike for that beautiful city and for the bathing girls of the Guadalquivir. However, I had to see some friends again and do some errands, which were to detain me at least three or four days in the old capital of the Moslem princes.

As soon as I reappeared at the Dominican monastery, one of the fathers, who had from the outset shown a lively interest in my research on the location of Munda, greeted me with open arms, exclaiming:

"Praised be the Lord! Welcome, my dear friend, welcome! All of us thought you were dead, and I, who am now speaking to you, have recited many *Paters* and *Aves*, which I don't regret, for the salvation of your soul. So you haven't been assassinated! We know, of course, that you've been robbed."

"Is that so?" I asked somewhat surprised.

"Yes. You know that fine watch with the repeating chimes that you used to make ring in the library when we told you that it was time to go to choir? Well, it's been recovered! It will be returned to you!"

"The fact is," I broke in, a bit abashed, "that I had lost it ..."

"The scoundrel is in safe custody, and, as it was known that he was the kind of man who would shoot down a Christian merely to rob him of a small coin, we were dying with fear that he might have killed you. I'll go with you to the *corregidor's* house, and we'll have your fine watch returned to you. And then just try to tell them in France that justice doesn't know its business in Spain!"

"I'll confess to you," I said to him, "that I'd prefer to lose my watch rather than give evidence that would cause a poor devil to be hanged, especially because ... because...."

"Oh, don't worry about that! He's been well recommended, and he cannot be hanged twice. When I say 'hanged', I'm wrong. This thief of yours is an *hidalgo*, a gentleman, so he'll be garrotted the day after tomorrow without reprieve.[11] You'll see that one theft more or less won't change anything in his case. Would to Heaven that he had only stolen! But he's committed several murders, each of them more horrible than the others."

"What's his name?" I asked.

"He's known in this part of the country by the name of José Navarro, but he also has another Basque name which neither you nor I will ever be able to pronounce. Yes indeed, he's a man worth seeing, and you, who love to discover the peculiarities of our country, mustn't miss the opportunity to learn how scoundrels in Spain depart from this world. He's in the chapel, and Father Martinez will take you there."

My Dominican insisted so strongly that I should see the preparations for the "vary preetty leetle hanging," that I could not get out of it. I went to see the prisoner, fortified with a package of cigars which, I hoped, would make him forgive my indiscretion.

I was shown in to Don José just at the time when he was

taking his meal. He nodded his head rather coldly and thanked me politely for the gift which I had brought for him. After he had counted the cigars in the package which I had put in his hands, he selected a certain number of them and returned the rest to me, observing that he had no need to take any more.

I asked him if I might soften his lot somewhat, either with a little money or by means of the influence of my friends. At first he shrugged his shoulders, smiling sadly; but soon, changing his mind, he asked me to have a mass said for the salvation of his soul.

"Would you," he added timidly, "would you be good enough to have another said for a person who has offended you?"

"Certainly, my dear fellow," I said, "but no one, as far as I know, has offended me in this country."

He took my hand and shook it solemnly. After a moment of silence, he continued:

"Dare I ask you to do another favor for me?... When you return to your country, perhaps you'll be passing through Navarre, at least you'll pass through Vitoria, which isn't very far away."

"Yes," I told him, "I'll certainly be passing through Vitoria, but it's not impossible that I'll make a detour in order to visit Pamplona, and for your sake I think that I would willingly make that detour."

"Well, if you go to Pamplona, you'll see more than one thing that will interest you...It's a beautiful city...I'll give you this medal (he showed me a small silver medal he was wearing around his neck), you'll wrap it in some paper... (he stopped a moment in order to master his emotion...), and you'll hand it over yourself or have it handed over by someone else to a good woman whose address I'll tell you. You will say that I'm dead, but you will not say how I died."

I promised to carry out his request. I saw him again the next day, and I spent part of the day with him. It is from his lips that I learned the sad tale that you are about to read.

Carmen – III

"I was born," he said, "in Elizondo, in the Batzan Valley. My name is Don José Lizzarrabengoa, and you know Spain well enough, sir, for my name to tell you at once that I am a Basque and come from an old Christian family. If I use the title *Don*, it's because I have a right to it, and, if I were in Elizondo, I would show you my genealogy on a parchment. They wanted me to dedicate my life to the Church and they made me study for the priesthood, but I was making little progress. I was too fond of playing handball: that's what ruined me. When we Navarrese play handball, we forget everything else. One day when I had won, a fellow from Alava picked a fight with me. We used our *maquilas*,[12] and again I won, but that made it necessary for me to leave the Basque country. I fell in with some dragoons, and I enlisted in the Almanza cavalry regiment.

"The people from our mountains learn the military profession quickly. I soon became a corporal, and I had been promised the rank of sergeant when, to my misfortune, they put me on guard duty at the tobacco factory in Seville. If you've ever been in Seville, you've probably seen that big building outside the ramparts, near the Guadalquivir. It seems to me that I can still see the main gate and the guardhouse nearby. When they are on duty, Spanish soldiers either play cards or sleep. But I, as a true-blue Navarrese, always tried to keep busy. I was making a chain with some brass wire to hold my priming needle. Suddenly my comrades said: 'There goes the bell. The girls are going to come back to work.'

"You probably know, sir, that fully four to five hundred women work in the tobacco factory. They are the ones who roll the cigars in a big room. Men are not allowed to enter this room without a permit from the Magistrate, because the women, especially the young ones, remove some of their clothing for comfort when it's hot. At the hour when the working-girls return after their dinner, many young men go to watch them pass by and make all kinds of remarks to them. There are very few of these damsels who will refuse a taffeta mantilla, and men who are fond of this type of fishing need only bend down in order to catch the fish.

"While the others were looking, I stayed on my bench near the gate. I was young then; I continually kept thinking of my region, and I concluded that there couldn't be any pretty girls without blue skirts and without braids falling over their shoulders.[13] Besides, Andalusian girls frightened me; I wasn't yet accustomed to their ways: always teasing, never a sensible word.

"So there I was minding my own business making my chain, when I heard some townspeople say: 'There's the *gitanilla!*' I looked up, and I saw her. It was a Friday, and I'll never forget it. I saw that same Carmen whom you know, at whose house I met you some months ago.

"She was wearing a very short red skirt which revealed white silk stockings with more than one hole in them, and dainty red morocco leather shoes tied with flame-colored ribbons. She wore her mantilla lowered in order to show off her shoulders and a big bouquet of acacia at the opening of her blouse. She also had an acacia flower in the corner of her mouth, and she walked swaying her hips like a filly on the Cordova stud farm. In my region, a woman decked out in a costume like that would have caused people to make the sign of the cross. But in Seville, every man made some spicy compliment to her about her appearance. She answered each one by casting enticing side glances round about, her hand on her hip, as brazen as the true gypsy she was. At first she didn't appeal to me, and I resumed my work. But she, following the habit of women and cats, which don't come when they're called and which do come when they're not called, stopped in front of me and started up a conversation.

" 'Pal,' she said to me in the Andalusian manner, 'would you like to give me your chain to hold the keys to my strongbox?'

" 'It's to hold my priming needle,' I answered her.

" 'Your priming needle!' she exclaimed laughing. 'Ah! the gentleman is making lace, since he needs needles.'

"Everyone who was there began to laugh, and I felt myself blushing and unable to find anything to say to her in reply.

" 'Come, sweetheart,' she continued, 'make me seven yards of black lace for a mantilla, needle-man of my heart!'

"And taking the acacia flower which she had in her mouth, she tossed it at me with her thumb, and it hit me right between my two eyes. Sir, that had an effect on me as if a bullet had hit me . . . I didn't know where to hide, and I stayed there as stiff as a board. When she had gone into the factory, I saw the acacia flower which had fallen to the ground between my feet. I don't know what got into me, but I picked it up without my comrades noticing me doing it, and I put it carefully in my jacket like a precious thing. My first blunder!

"Two or three hours later I was still thinking about it, when a porter came running into the guardhouse, out of breath and looking very upset. He told us that a woman had been murdered in the big room of the cigar factory, and that the guard would have to be sent in. The sergeant told me to take two men and to investigate what had happened. I took my two men and went up. Just imagine, sir, after I had entered the room, I found first of all three hundred women in their slips and little else, all of them screaming, howling, gesticulating, making such a racket that one couldn't even have heard God's thunder. On one side there was one of them flat on her back, covered with blood and with an X on her face which had been made shortly before by two slashes with a knife. In front of the wounded woman, to whom the better ones of the group were lending their help, I saw Carmen, held in check by five or six of her fellow workers. The wounded woman was screaming: 'Confession! Confession! I'm dying!' Carmen said nothing. She clenched her teeth and rolled her eyes like a chameleon.

" 'What's this all about?' I asked.

"I had a great deal of trouble finding out just what had taken place, for all the women were talking to me at the same time in their excitement. It seemed that the wounded woman had boasted that she had enough money in her pocket to buy a donkey in the market at Triana. 'Oh, shut up,' said Carmen, who had a sharp tongue in her head, 'isn't a broom good enough for you any more?'[14] The other woman, hurt by the reproach, perhaps because she felt dubious about the mentioned article, answered that she was not familiar with brooms, not having the honor to be either a gypsy woman or the godchild of Satan. She added that Señorita Carmencita would soon enough make the acquaintance of her donkey, when his Honor, the *Corregidor,* took her out for a ride with two flunkeys behind them to chase away the flies. 'Well now, I'll have to prepare you for that pleasure,' said Carmen. 'I'll have to make some drinking troughs for the flies on your cheek. I'm going to paint a checkerboard on it this very minute.'[15] Thereupon, swish! slash! with the knife which she used to cut the ends of the cigars, Carmen started to carve the Cross of Saint Andrew on her face.

"The case was clear. I seized Carmen by the arm.

" 'Sister,' I said to her politely, 'you'll have to come with me.' She cast a glance at me as she recognized me, but she said in a resigned tone of voice: 'Very well, let's get going! Where is my mantilla?' She placed it on her head in such a way as to show only one of her big eyes, and followed my two men as gentle as a lamb.

"When we arrived at the guardhouse, the sergeant said that it was a serious matter and that she had to be taken to prison. Again, I was the one who had to take her there. I placed her between two dragoons and I marched in the rear, as a corporal must do on such occasions. We started off for the city. At first the gypsy girl kept silent, but in Serpent Street—which, as you know, well deserves its name because of the many turns that it has—in Serpent Street she started off by letting her mantilla slip down on her shoulders in order to reveal her cajoling little face, and, turning toward me as much as she could, she said to me:

" 'Officer, where are you taking me?'

" 'To prison, my poor child,' I answered her as gently as I could, as a good soldier must speak to a prisoner, especially to a woman.

" 'Alas, what will become of me? Please, officer, have pity on me. You're so young, so nice'...(Then, in a softer tone of voice): 'Let me escape,' she said, 'I'll give you a piece of the *bar lachi,* which will make you loved by all women.'

"The *bar lachi,* sir, is the lodestone with which gypsies claim one can cast a great number of spells, when one knows how to use it. Have a woman drink a glass of white wine with a little scraped into it, and she will no longer resist your advances. I answered her as seriously as I could:

" 'We're not here to talk about silly things. You must go to prison, that's the order, and there's nothing that we can do about it.'

"We people of the Basque country have an accent which makes us easily recognizable from the Spaniards. On the other hand, there isn't one of them who can even learn to say *baï, jaona.*[1'] Carmen, therefore, had no trouble in guessing that I came from the Provinces. You must know, sir, that the gypsies, being from no country of their own and being continually on the move, speak all languages. Most of them are quite at home in Portugal, in France, in the Provinces, in Catalonia—everywhere; even with the Moors and the English they make themselves understood. Consequently, Carmen knew the Basque language quite well.

" *'Laguna ene bihotsarena,* comrade of my heart,' she said to me suddenly, 'are you from the Basque country?'

"Our language, sir, is so beautiful, that, when we hear it in a foreign land, it gives us a thrill...I'd like to have a father confessor from the Provinces,"[17] the bandit added more softly.

He continued after a silence:

" 'I'm from Elizondo,' I answered her in Basque, very moved to hear her speaking my language.

" 'I'm from Etchalar,' she said. (That's a district four hours away from my home.) 'I was carried away by some gypsies to Seville. I worked in the factory to earn enough in order to return to Navarre, for I wanted to be with my poor mother who has no one but me to support her and a little *barratcea*[18] with twenty apple trees for cider. Ah! If only I were back in the Basque country, standing before the white mountain! They have insulted me here because I'm not from this land of crooks and sellers of rotten oranges; these wenches, sir, have all turned against me, because I've told them that all their Seville *jacques*[19] with their knives wouldn't frighten one stout-hearted lad from home with his blue beret and his *maquila*. Comrade, dear friend, won't you do something for a fellow countrywoman?'

"She was lying, sir, she's always lied. I don't know if that girl has ever spoken a word of truth in her whole life. But when she spoke, I believed her: I couldn't help it. She murdered the Basque language, and still I believed that she was from Navarre. Only her eyes and her mouth and her complexion stamped her as a gypsy. I was crazy; I no longer paid attention to anything else. I thought that if some Spaniards had taken it into their heads to speak ill of my country, I too would have cut up their faces just as she had done to her comrade. In short, I was like a drunken man. I was beginning to say some silly things, and I was very near to acting that way too.

" 'If I were to push you and you were to fall down, countryman,' she continued in Basque, 'I guarantee that these two Castilian draftees couldn't hold me.'

"By my faith, I forgot all about the order and everything else, and I said to her:

" 'Well, my dear countrywoman, try it, and may Our Lady of the Mountain come to your aid!'

"At that moment we were passing by one of those narrow alleys of which there are so many in Seville. Suddenly Carmen turned around and with her fist punched me in the chest. I allowed myself to fall backward on purpose. In one bound she jumped over me and began to run showing us a pair of pretty legs!...They talk about 'Basque legs': hers were certainly quite equal to any I've ever seen...as fast as they were shapely. I got up immediately, but I placed my lance[20] crosswise, in such a way as to block the street...so well, that at the very outset my comrades were stopped as they began to pursue her. Then I myself began to run, and they came running behind me. But try to catch up with her! There wasn't a chance with our spurs, our sabers, and our lances! In less time than it's taking me to tell you about it, the prisoner had disappeared. Besides, all the women of the neighborhood helped her in her flight, poked fun at us, and gave us the wrong directions. After several marches and countermarches, we had to go back to the guardhouse without a receipt from the governor of the prison.

"My men, in order not to be punished, said that Carmen had spoken Basque to me and that it didn't seem very natural, to tell the truth, that a punch from such a little girl should so easily knock down a strapping fellow with my strength. It all seemed highly suspicious or, rather, too obvious. At the changing of the guard I was stripped of my rank and sent to prison for a month. It was my first punishment since I had been in the service. Goodbye to the sergeant's stripes I thought were already mine!

"My first days in prison passed very sadly. On joining the army, I had imagined that at the very least I would get to be an officer. Longa and Mina, my fellow countrymen, are now full captains-general; Chapalangarra, who, like Mina, is a Negro, is also like him a refugee in your country. Chapalangarra used to be a colonel, and I've played handball scores of times with his brother, who was a poor devil just like me. Now I said to myself: 'All the time that you've served so far without punishment is time lost. There you are now with a black mark against you! To get yourself back in the good graces of your superior officers, you'll have to work ten times harder than you did when you first came in as a recruit! And why did I expose myself to punishment? For a gypsy wench who has made a fool of me, and who at this very moment is busy stealing in some corner of the town.' However, I couldn't stop thinking of her! Would you believe it, sir? I saw continually before my eyes her torn silk stockings, which she had exposed to me so freely when fleeing. I looked through the bars of my prison into the street and, among all the women who passed by, I didn't see a single one who was worth that devil of a girl! And then, in spite of myself, I smelled the acacia flower which she had tossed to me and which, though withered, continued to keep its sweet aroma . . . If there really are any witches, sir, that girl certainly was one!

"One day the jailor came into my cell and gave me a loaf of Alcalá bread.[21]

" 'Here,' he said to me, 'look what your cousin has sent you.'

"I took the bread, very much surprised, for I had no cousin in

Seville. 'Perhaps it's a mistake,' I thought, while looking at the bread. But it was so appetizing and it smelled so good that, without worrying about where it came from and for whom it was meant, I made up my mind to eat it. When I attempted to cut it, my knife came upon something hard. I looked more closely and found a little English file which someone had slipped into the dough before the bread was baked. In the loaf there was also a two-piastre gold coin. There was no doubt about it: it was a gift from Carmen! For people of her race, liberty is everything, and they would set a town on fire in order to spare themselves one day in prison. Besides, the girl was smart, and with a loaf of bread like this, one could laugh at any jailor.

"In an hour, the thickest bar would be sawed through with the little file, and with the two-piastre gold piece I would change the overcoat of my uniform for civilian clothing at the first old clothes shop. You can easily imagine that a man who had many times taken young eaglets from their nest in our mountains was hardly embarrassed by having to climb down into the street from a window less than thirty feet above the ground; but I didn't want to escape. I still had my sense of honor as a soldier, and to desert seemed to me a great crime. But I was touched by this sign of remembrance on Carmen's part. When a man is in prison, he likes to think that he's got a friend on the outside who's interested in him. The gold coin embarrassed me a bit and I would have liked very much to return it, but where was I to find my creditor? That didn't seem an easy matter to me.

"After the ceremony of my demotion, I thought I had nothing more to suffer, but there remained yet another humiliation for me to swallow. It was on my leaving prison, when I was ordered to duty and put on guard as a lowly private. You just can't imagine what a sensitive man feels on an occasion such as that! I believe I would have preferred to be shot. As a corporal, at least a man marches alone, at the head of his squad; he feels that he is somebody; people look up to him!

"I was put on sentry duty at the colonel's door. He was a rich young man, a good fellow, who liked to have some fun. All the young officers were at his house as well as many civilians, including some women: actresses, so people said. As far as I was concerned, it seemed to me that the whole city had arranged to meet at his door in order to look at me. Then along came the colonel's carriage with his manservant on the seat. And who stepped out before my eyes? . . . the *gitanilla*. This time she was adorned like a shrine, all dressed up and bedecked with gold ribbons! She was wearing a dress with spangles, blue shoes also with spangles, and flowers and gold braid everywhere! In her hand she had a Basque tambourine. There were two other gypsies with her, one a young girl and the other an old woman. There's always an old woman to lead them; then there's an old man, also a gypsy, with a guitar, to play and make them dance. You know that people often seek entertainment by having gypsies come to social functions in order to have them dance their gypsy dance, the *romalis*, and often to do many other things.

"Carmen recognized me, and we exchanged glances. I don't know why, but at that moment I'd gladly have been a hundred feet under the ground.

" '*Agur laguna*,'²² she said. 'Officer, you're standing guard like a draftee!'

"And, before I'd found a word to answer her, she was in the house.

"The whole party was in the patio, and, in spite of the crowd, I saw just about everything that went on through the grilled gate.²³ I heard the castanets, the drum, the laughter and the bravos; at times I would see her head when she jumped with her drum. Then I also heard some officers saying many things to her which brought a flush to my face. What she answered them, I don't know. I think it was from that day onward that I really began to love her, for the idea occurred to me three or four times to enter the patio and plunge my saber into the bellies of all those young whippersnappers who were flirting with her. My torture lasted a full hour; then the gypsies came out and the carriage took them away. Carmen, as she passed by, looked at me again with the eyes that you already know, and said to me in a very low voice: 'Countryman, when people love good fried food, they go to eat in Triana, at Lillas Pastia's place.'

"As light-footed as a kid, she dashed into the carriage. The coachman whipped up his mules, and the whole merry band drove off I know not where.

"You can easily guess that I went to Triana when I came off guard duty, but first of all I got a shave and then I brushed myself as if it were for a parade day. She was at the establishment of Lillas Pastia, an old vendor of fried foods, a gypsy as black as a Moor, to whose inn many townsfolk came to eat fried fish, especially, I think, since Carmen had taken up her quarters there.

" 'Lillas,' she said, as soon as she saw me, 'I'm not doing any more today. Tomorrow will be another day.²⁴ Come, countryman, let's go for a walk.'

"She drew her mantilla in front of her face, and there we were on the street, without my knowing where I was going.

" 'Young lady,' I said to her, 'I believe that I have you to thank for a gift which you sent me when I was in prison. I ate the bread; the file will serve me to sharpen my lance, and I'll keep it as a souvenir from you; but as for the money, here it is.'

" 'Well, what do you know, he's kept the money intact,' she exclaimed and burst out laughing. 'Well, so much the better, for I'm very short of funds. But what of that? A stray dog never dies of hunger.²⁵ Come on, let's go on a spending spree! Let's eat up all of it! You'll treat me!'

"We had taken the road leading back to Seville. At the entrance to Serpent Street, she bought a dozen oranges, which she had me wrap in my handkerchief. A little farther on, she also bought a loaf of bread, some sausage, and a bottle of manzanilla. Then, finally, she entered a confectioner's shop. There, she threw on the counter the gold coin which I'd given back to her, plus another one that she had in her pocket, along with some silver coins. She also asked me to give her all the change I had. I found only a small coin and a few *cuartos* in my pockets, which I handed over to her, greatly ashamed that I hadn't any more. I thought that she wanted to buy out the whole shop. She picked all the finest and the most expensive things that were there—*yemas*,²⁶ *turón*,²⁷ candied fruits—as long as the money lasted. I had to carry all that too, in paper bags.

"Perhaps you know Candilejo Street, where there is a bust of

King Pedro the Just.[28] It should have inspired me to think a bit about it. We stopped in this street before an old house. She went into the entryway and knocked at the ground floor door. A gypsy woman, a true servant of Satan, came to open the door. Carmen said some words to her in *Romany*.[29] At first the old woman grumbled. To appease her, Carmen gave her two oranges and a handful of candy, and let her have a taste of the wine. Then she put the old woman's cloak on her back and led her to the door, which she closed with the wooden bar. As soon as we were alone, she began to dance and to laugh like a madwoman, singing:

" 'You're my *rom*, I'm your *romi*.'[30]

"I stood in the middle of the room, loaded with all her purchases not knowing where to put them. She dropped everything to the floor, and, throwing her arms about my neck, she said to me:

" 'I pay my debts! I pay my debts! That's the law of the *Calés*!'[31]

"Ah, sir, what a day! What a day! ... When I think of it, I forget all about tomorrow."

The bandit fell silent for a moment. Then, after relighting his cigar, he continued:

"We spent the whole day together, eating, drinking, and the rest. When she had eaten some of the candy like a six-year-old child, she stuffed handfuls of it into the old woman's water-jar. 'That's to make herself some sherbet,' she said. She smashed some *yemas* by throwing them against the wall. 'That's so the flies won't pester us,' she said. There wasn't a trick or a prank that she didn't play. I told her that I'd like to see her dance, but where were castanets to be found? Did that stop Carmen? Not at all. She promptly took the old woman's only plate, broke it into two pieces, and there she was, dancing the *romalis*[32] for me, making the pieces of crockery clack just as well as if she'd had castanets made of ebony or ivory. A man wasn't bored with that girl, that's for sure! Evening came and I heard the drums sounding tattoo.

" 'I must go to my barracks now for roll call,' I told her.

" 'To your barracks?' she said, looking at me with disdain.
'So you're a Negro slave and allow yourself to be prodded with a
stick! You're a real canary all right, in dress and in character![33]
Go on, then! You're chicken-hearted!'

"I stayed, resigned beforehand that I'd end up in the
guardhouse. In the morning, she was the one who first spoke of
our parting.

" 'Listen to me, my little José,' she said, 'have I paid you
back? According to our law, I owed you nothing, since you're my
payllo. But you're a handsome fellow, and you've pleased me.
We're even. Good-bye.'

"I asked her when I'd see her again.

" 'When you're not such a big ninny,' she replied laughing.
Then in a more serious tone of voice, she said: 'Do you know
what, my boy? I think I love you a little. But that can't last. A dog
and a wolf don't make a good household for long.[34] Perhaps if
you'd be willing to follow the law of the gypsies, I'd be willing
to become your *romi.* But these are silly ideas; that can't
be. Ah, my boy, believe me, you're getting off very cheaply.
You've met up with the Devil, yes, the Devil,—he's not always
black, you know—and he hasn't twisted your neck. I wear a
woolen dress, but I'm no sheep.[35] Go and light a candle to your
majari,[36] she's well earned it. So, go away! Good-bye once more!
Think no more of Carmencita, or she'll make you marry a widow
with wooden legs.'[37]

"While speaking in this manner, she was removing the bar
which bolted the door, and, once on the street, she wrapped
herself in her mantilla and turned her heels on me.

"She was speaking the truth. I would have been wise not to
think of her any more, but since that day in Candilejo Street I
could no longer think of anything else. I wandered around all day
long hoping to meet her. I asked the old woman and the fried food
vendor for news of her. Both of them replied that she had left for
Laloro;[38] that's what they call Portugal. Probably they answered
in this fashion in accordance with instructions given to them by
Carmen, but it didn't take me long to discover that they were
lying. Some weeks after my day on Candilejo Street, I was on

sentry duty at one of the city gates. A short distance from this gate, there was a breach which had been made in the surrounding wall. Work was carried on at this breach during the day, and at night a sentry was posted there to stop smugglers. During the working hours in the daytime I saw Lillas Pastia walking back and forth around the guardhouse and talking to some of my comrades. All of them knew him, and his fish and his doughnuts even better. He came up to me and asked me if I had had any news of Carmen.

" 'No,' I told him.

" 'Well, you'll get some soon, my friend,' he replied.

"He wasn't mistaken. That night I was put on sentry duty at the breach, and, as soon as the corporal had withdrawn, I saw a woman coming toward me. My heart told me that it was Carmen. Nevertheless, I shouted:

" 'Away with you! You can't pass!'

" 'Oh, don't be so nasty,' she said, making herself known to me.

" 'What! So it's you, Carmen!'

" 'Yes, my countryman! Let's be brief and to the point. Do you want to earn a *douro*? Some people will be coming along with packages. Let them go on their way.'

" 'No,' I answered, 'I must prevent them from passing through. Those are my orders.'

" 'Your orders! Your orders! You didn't think about them in Candilejo Street.'

" 'Ah!' I replied, much upset by the mere memory, 'that was certainly worth forgetting my orders, but I don't want any money from smugglers.'

" 'Well, then, let's see! If you don't want any money, do you want to have dinner with me again at old Dorothea's place?'

" 'No,' I said, half choked by the effort I was making, 'I can't.'

" 'Very well, then. If you're going to be so difficult, I know whom I'll ask. I'll make your officer an offer to go to Dorothea's place with him. He seems to be a good fellow, and he'll assign as a sentinel a fellow who won't see anymore than he should.

Good-bye, canary, I'll really laugh the day when the orders are to hang you.'

"I was weak enough to call her back, and I promised to allow every gypsy in the world to pass through, if necessary, provided that I'd get the only reward that I desired. She swore to me at once that she'd keep her word the very next day, and then ran to notify her friends, who were a few paces away. There were five of them, among them Pastia, all heavily laden with English merchandise. Carmen stood watch. She was supposed to warn them with her castanets as soon as she saw the patrol making its rounds, but she didn't need to do so. The smugglers finished their work in no time at all.

"The next day I went to Candilejo Street. Carmen kept me waiting and finally came out in quite a bad humor.

" 'I don't like people who have to be begged,' she said. 'You did me a greater favor the first time, without knowing if you'd get anything in return. Yesterday you bargained with me. I don't know why I've come, for I don't love you any more. So there, go away! Here's a *douro* for your trouble.'

"It would have taken very little for me to fling the coin in her face, and I had to make a strong effort to restrain myself from beating her. After arguing for an hour, I was furious and left her. I wandered through the city for some time, walking aimlessly here and there like a madman. Finally I entered a church, and, sitting down in the darkest corner, I wept bitter tears. Suddenly I heard a voice:

" 'Dragon[39] tears! I'd like to make a love potion with them!'

"I raised my eyes. It was Carmen who was standing before me.

" 'Well, countryman, are you still angry with me?' she said to me. 'I must certainly be in love with you, in spite of being mad at you, for since you left me I don't know what's wrong with me. Well, now I'm the one who's asking you if you'd like to come with me to Candilejo Street.'

"So we made our peace, but Carmen had moods like the weather. Never is a storm so near in our mountains as when the sun is at its brightest. Another time she had promised to see me again at Dorothea's place, and she didn't come. Dorothea told me very courteously that she had gone to Portugal on gypsy business.

"Knowing from past experience how much to rely upon that, I looked for Carmen everywhere I could think of that she might be. I walked down Candilejo Street a score of times each day. One evening I had again dropped in at Dorothea's place (I had almost tamed the old woman by buying her a glass of anisette from time to time), when Carmen entered, followed by a young man, a lieutenant in my regiment.

" 'Get out of here fast,' she said to me in Basque.

"Dumbfounded, I stood there with rage in my heart.

" 'What are you doing here?' the lieutenant said to me. 'Clear out! Get out of here at once!'

"I couldn't take a step. My legs seemed to be paralysed. The officer, furious when he saw that I wasn't leaving and that I hadn't even taken off my military cap, took hold of me by the collar and shook me roughly. I don't remember what I said to him. He drew his sword and I unsheathed mine. The old woman seized my arm, and the lieutenant struck me with a blow on the forehead from which I still bear the scar. I drew back, and, with one thrust of my elbow, I threw Dorothea to the floor. Then, as the lieutenant was coming at me, I put the point of my sword to his body and he ran himself through. Carmen then put out the lamp, and in her language she told Dorothea to flee. As for me, I escaped into the street and began to run without knowing where to go. It seemed to me that someone was following me. When at last I came to my senses, I found that Carmen hadn't left me.

" 'You big stupid canary!' she said to me, 'all you can do is make blunders! Well, I told you that I'd bring you bad luck. But come with me; let's get out of this mess! There's a remedy for all things when one has a Fleming from Rome[40] as his sweetheart. Begin by tying this handkerchief around your head, and throw that sword belt of yours to me. Wait for me in this alley. I'll be back in a few minutes.'

"She disappeared and soon returned, bringing back with her a striped cloak which she had gone to fetch I don't know where.

She made me take off my uniform and put on the cloak over my shirt. Dressed in this manner, along with the handkerchief she had used to bandage the wound on my forehead, I looked rather like the Valencian peasants one sees in Seville, who come there to sell their syrup of *chufas*.[41] Then she took me into a house quite similar to Dorothea's place, at the end of a little lane. She and another gypsy woman washed and dressed my wound better than an army surgeon could have done, and made me swallow some sort of drink. Finally they placed me on a mattress, and I fell sound asleep.

"Probably these women had mixed into my drink some of those sleep-inducing drugs whose secret they know, for I didn't wake up until very late the following day. I had a severe headache and a slight fever. It took me some time to recall the terrible scene in which I had taken part the evening before. After they had dressed my wound, Carmen and her friend, the gypsy woman, both squatted on their heels beside my mattress and exchanged some words in *chippe calli*[42] which seemed to be a medical consultation. Then both of them assured me that I would be completely cured in a short time, but that I must leave Seville as soon as possible, for if I were caught there I'd be shot without mercy.

" 'My boy,' Carmen said to me, 'now you must do something else for a living, because the king is no longer giving you either rice or dried codfish.[43] You must think about another career. You're too stupid to steal *a pastesas*[44] but you're agile and strong. If you have the heart for it, go away to the coast and become a smuggler. Didn't I promise you that I'd cause you to be hanged? That's better than being shot. Besides, if you know how to go about it, you'll live like a prince, as long as the *miñons*[45] and the coast guards don't collar you.'

"It was in this engaging fashion that that devil of a girl described to me the new career she intended for me, the only one, to tell the truth, which was left to me now that I had incurred the death penalty. Need I tell you, sir, that she convinced me without much difficulty? It seemed to me that I was attaching myself to her more closely by this life of danger and rebellion. Henceforth,

I thought I could be sure of her love. I had often heard people talk of smugglers who roamed Andalusia, each mounted on a good horse, musket in hand and his mistress riding behind him. I already saw myself trotting up hill and down dale with the lovely gypsy behind me. When I spoke to her about that, she almost split her sides laughing and told me that there's nothing so fine as a night spent in bivouac, when each *rom* retires with his *romi* under his little tent, made of a blanket over three hoops.

" 'If I ever get you into the mountains,' I said to her, 'I'll be sure of you! There won't be any lieutenant there to share you with me.'

" 'Ah! You're jealous!' she replied. 'So much the worse for you! How is it you're so stupid about that? Don't you see that I love you, since I've never asked you for money?'

"When she talked that way, I felt like strangling her.

"To make a long story short, sir, Carmen got civilian clothes for me, in which I left Seville without being recognized. I went to Jerez with a letter from Pastia to an anisette dealer, at whose place some smugglers used to meet. I was introduced to those people, whose leader, nicknamed Dancaïre, accepted me into his band. We left for Gaucin, where I again found Carmen, who had arranged a rendezvous with me there. On our expeditions she served as a spy for our people, and there never was a better one. She was on her way back from Gibraltar, and she had already arranged with a ship's skipper to take aboard English merchandise which we were to receive on the coast. We went to wait for it near Estepona, then we hid a portion of it in the mountains. Laden with the rest, we made our way to Ronda. Carmen had gone there before us, and again it was she who indicated the exact moment when we should enter the town. This first trip and some others after it were happy ones. I liked the life of a smuggler better than the life of a soldier. I gave gifts to Carmen. I had money and a mistress. I felt scarcely any remorse, for, as the gypsies say: When there's pleasure, a scab doesn't itch.[46]

"We were well received everywhere. My companions treated me well and even showed me some consideration. The reason was that I had killed a man, and there were some among them who didn't have a similar exploit on their conscience. But what pleased me even more in my new life was that I saw Carmen often. She showed me more affection than ever; however, in front of our comrades, she didn't agree that she was my mistress, and she even made me swear all sorts of oaths that I would tell them nothing concerning her. I was so weak before that creature that I obeyed her in all her whims. Besides, it was the first time she revealed the modesty of a decent woman, and I was simple enough to believe that she had really given up her former ways.

"Our troop, which was composed of eight or ten men, hardly ever met, except at decisive moments. Ordinarily, we were scattered by twos and threes in the towns and villages. Each of us pretended to have a trade: this one was a tinsmith, that one a horse dealer. As for me, I was a haberdashery merchant, but I scarcely ever showed my face in the big towns because of my trouble in Seville. One day, or rather one night, our meeting place was in lower Vejer.[47] Dancaïre and I were there before the others. He seemed very gay.

" 'We're going to have one more comrade now,' he told me. 'Carmen has just played one of her best tricks. She's helped her *rom*, who was in the presidio at Tarifa,[47] to escape.'

"I was already beginning to understand the gypsy language, which almost all of my comrades spoke, and this word *rom* gave me a shock.

" 'What! Her husband! Then she's married?' I asked the captain.

" 'Yes,' he replied, 'to García One Eye, a gypsy who's just as slippery as she is. The poor fellow was condemned to the galleys. Carmen bamboozled the surgeon of the presidio so well, that she was able to obtain the freedom of her *rom*. Ah! That girl is worth her weight in gold! She's been trying to arrange his escape for the past two years. Nothing was successful until the moment when they decided to change the chief medical officer. With the latter it certainly seems that she has found the means of coming to an agreement very quickly.'

"You can well imagine the pleasure that this news gave me. I soon met García One Eye, who was without a doubt the ugliest monster ever produced by the gypsy race. With a dark skin and blacker soul, he was the most arrant scoundrel I've ever met in my life. Carmen came back to us with him, and, when she called him her *rom* in front of me, you should have seen the eyes she made at me, and then her grimaces when García turned his head. I was furious and I didn't speak to her all night. In the morning, we had made up our bundles and were already on our way, when we noticed that about a dozen horsemen were on our heels. The boastful Andalusians, who usually talked only of slaughtering everything, now immediately had a pitiful expression on their faces. There was a general scramble: every man for himself. Dancaïre, García, a handsome young fellow from Ecija named Remendado, and Carmen didn't lose their heads. The rest had abandoned the mules and dashed into the ravines, where the horses couldn't follow them.

"We couldn't take our animals along with us, and so we hastened to untie the best of our loot and to load it on our shoulders. Then we tried to escape over the rocks, down the steepest slopes. We threw our bundles before us and followed them as best we could, sliding on our heels. All this time the enemy was sniping at us. It was the first time that I had heard the whistling of bullets so close to me, but it didn't impress me much. When a man is in a woman's presence, there's no merit in making fun of death. All of us escaped except poor Remendado, who was hit in the back. I threw down my bundle and tried to pick him up.

" 'Imbecile,' García yelled at me, 'what do we want witn carrion? Finish him off, and don't leave his cotton stockings behind!'

" 'Drop him!' Carmen shouted at me.

"Weariness made it necessary for me to put him down for a moment in the shelter of a rock. García came up with his musket and blasted him in the head.

" 'He's a very clever man indeed who'd recognize him how,' he said, looking at his face, which twelve bullets had blown to bits.

"That, sir, is the fine life I led. In the evening, we found ourselves in a thicket, exhausted with fatigue, with nothing to eat, and ruined by the loss of our mules. What did that devil García do then? He pulled a pack of cards out of his pocket and began to play with Dancaïre by the glow of a fire which they had lit. During this time, I was lying down looking at the stars, thinking of Remendado, and saying to myself that I'd just as soon be in his place. Carmen was crouching near me, and, from time to time, she would clack her castanets as she hummed. Then, coming close to me as if to whisper in my ear, she kissed me, almost in spite of myself, two or three times.

" 'You are the very devil,' I told her.

" 'Yes,' she replied.

"After a few hours of rest, she went off to Gaucín, and the next morning a little goatherd came and brought us some bread. We stayed there the whole day, and at night we went on closer to Gaucín. We were waiting for word from Carmen. Nothing came. At dawn we saw a muleteer accompanying a well-dressed woman with a parasol and a little girl, who seemed to be her maid. García said to us:

" 'There are two mules and two women that Saint Nicholas is sending us. I'd prefer four mules, but, no matter, I'll make do with them.'

"He took his musket and went down toward the path, hiding in the shrubs. Dancaïre and I followed at a short distance behind him. When we were within shooting distance, we showed ourselves and shouted at the mule driver to stop. The woman, when she saw us, instead of being afraid—and our appearance should have been sufficient for that—burst our laughing.

" 'Ah, what *lillipendi*,' she said. 'They take me for an *erañi*!' [48]

"It was Carmen, but she was so well disguised that I wouldn't have recognized her if she had spoken any other language. She jumped down from her mule and chatted for a while in an undertone with Dancaïre and García. Then she said to me:

" 'Canary bird, we'll see each other again before you're

hanged. I'm going to Gibraltar now on gypsy business. You'll soon hear from me.'

"We separated after she had indicated a place where we could find a shelter for a few days. That girl was the salvation of our band. Soon we received some money which she sent to us, and information which was worth even more: on a certain day and by a certain road, two English lords would leave Gibraltar for Granada. A word to the wise is sufficient. They had a great number of guineas with them. García wanted to kill them, but Dancaïre and I were against it. We took from them only their money and their watches, besides their shirts, which we badly needed for ourselves.

"Sir, a man becomes a scoundrel without even meaning to. A pretty girl makes him lose his head. He fights for her, an accident happens, he's forced to live in the mountains, and from a smuggler he becomes a bandit before he knows it. We decided that it wasn't healthy for us in the vicinity of Gibraltar after the affair with the English lords, and so we plunged into the Sierra de Ronda. You've spoken to me of José María. Well, that's where I made his acquaintance. He took his mistress on his expeditions. She was a pretty girl, sensible, modest, and well-mannered. Never a coarse word, and such deep devotion!...In return, he made her very unhappy. He was always running after all the girls; he mistreated her; then, sometimes he decided to play jealous. Once he even slashed her with his knife. Well, she merely loved him the more for it. Women are made that way, especially Andalusian women. That one was proud of the scar which she had on her arm and showed it off to everyone as the most beautiful thing in the world. On top of all that, José María was, moreover, the worst of comrades!...On one of our expeditions, he arranged matters so well for himself that all the profit went to him and we had the fighting and the trouble in the affair. But I must get back to my story. We heard no further news of Carmen. Dancaïre said:

" 'One of us must go to Gibraltar to get some news of her. She must have arranged some business. I'd be willing to go, but I'm too well known in Gibraltar.'

"García One Eye said:

" 'So am I. They know me there too, for I've played so many tricks on the English lobsters.[49] And, as I've got only one eye, I'm a hard man to disguise.'

" 'Then I suppose I'll have to go,' I said in my turn, delighted at the mere thought of seeing Carmen again. 'Tell me, what must I do?'

The others said to me:

" 'Either go by boat or by way of San Roque, as you prefer, and when you reach Gibraltar, ask at the port where a woman chocolate vendor named La Rollona lives. When you've found her, you'll find out from her what's going on over there.'

"It was agreed that all three of us would set out for the Sierra de Gaucín, where I'd leave my two companions and make my way to Gibraltar as a fruit vendor. At Ronda, a man who was one of us had procured a passport for me; at Gaucín, they gave me a donkey. I loaded it with oranges and melons, and then I set out on my way. When I arrived at Gibraltar, I found that La Rollona was well known there, but that she was either dead or had gone off *ad finibus terrae.*[50] Her disappearance, in my opinion, explained why we had lost our means of communicating with Carmen. I put my donkey in a stable, and, taking along my oranges, I went through the town pretending to sell them, but my real reason was to see if I might not perchance meet up with a familiar face. There are many scoundrels there from every land, and it's a veritable Tower of Babel. A person can't take ten steps in that place without hearing as many languages spoken. I saw many gypsies, but I hardly dared to trust them. I sounded them out, and they sounded me out. We guessed quite definitely that we were fellow rogues; the important thing was to find out if we belonged to the same band.

"After two days spent in useless walking about, I'd learned nothing concerning either La Rollona or Carmen. I was thinking of returning to my comrades after I'd done a little shopping when, strolling along the street at sunset, I heard a woman's voice from a window above calling to me: 'Orange vendor!...' I raised my head, and, on a balcony, I saw Carmen leaning on her elbows, and beside her a curly-headed officer in a red uniform with golden epaulettes, who had the appearance of a great English lord. As for Carmen, whe was superbly dressed all in silk, a shawl over her shoulders, a golden comb in her hair. As always, that fine girl was acting out a comedy and was laughing to split her sides. The Englishman, speaking broken Spanish, shouted to me to come up because the lady wanted some oranges, and Carmen said to me in Basque:

" 'Come on up, and don't be surprised at anything you see.'

"Nothing, in fact, could surprise me where she was concerned. I don't know whether I was more joyous than angry at finding her again. At the door there was a tall, powdered English servant, who led me into a magnificent salon. Carmen immediately said to me in Basque:

" 'You don't know a word of Spanish, and you don't know me.'

"Then, turning to the Englishman:

" 'It's just as I told you. I recognized him at once as a Basque. You're going to hear what a funny language he speaks. How silly he looks, doesn't he? One might almost say like a cat surprised in the larder.'

" 'And you,' I said to her in my language, 'you look like a brazen hussy, and I'd really like to slash your face in front of your lover.'

" 'My lover!' she exclaimed. 'Come now! Tell me, did you guess all that by yourself? And you're really jealous of this imbecile here? You're even a bigger fool than before our evenings in Condilejo Street. Don't you see, dolt that you are, that at this very moment I'm conducting gypsy business, and in the most brilliant fashion? This house is mine, and this lobster's guineas will be mine. I lead him around by the nose, and I'll lead him to a place where he'll never get out.'

" 'Now you listen to me,' I said, 'if you ever do your gypsy business again in this fashion, I'll fix you so thoroughly that you'll never try it on anyone else!'

" 'Ah! Really now! Are you my *rom* to order me about? One Eye thinks it's all right, so what business is it of yours? Shouldn't you be very happy that you're the only man who can call himself my *minchorrô?'* [51]

" 'What's that he's saying?' asked the Englishman.

" 'He says he's thirsty and that he'd like very much to have something to drink,' answered Carmen. Then she threw herself back on a sofa, bursting out laughing at her translation.

"Sir, when that girl laughed, there was just no way to talk sense. Everyone laughed with her. That big Englishman also began to laugh, like the imbecile he was, and ordered the servant to bring me something to drink.

"While I was drinking, Carmen said:

" 'Do you see that ring he's wearing on his finger? If you want it, I'll give it to you.'

"But I replied:

" 'I'd give my finger to have your lord up in my mountains, with each of us holding a *maquila.'* [52]

" *'Maquila,* what does that mean?' asked the Englishman.

" *'Maquila,'* said Carmen, continually laughing, 'that's an orange. Isn't that a very funny word for an orange? He says he'd like to have you eat a *maquila.'*

" 'Yes?' said the Englishman. 'Well, bring some more *maquilas* tomorrow.'

"While we were talking, the servant entered and said that dinner was ready. Then the Englishman got up, gave me a piastre, and offered his arm to Carmen, as if she couldn't walk alone. Carmen, constantly laughing, said to me:

" 'My boy, I can't invite you to dinner, but tomorrow, as soon as you hear the drum for the parade, come here with your oranges. You'll find a room that's better furnished than the one in Candilejo Street, and you'll see whether or not I'm still your Carmencita. And then we'll talk about gypsy business.'

"I didn't answer, and I was already outside on the street, when the Englishman shouted down to me:

" 'Bring some *maquilas* tomorrow!' And I heard Carmen's peals of laughter.

"I went away, not knowing what I'd do. I hardly slept, and, in the morning, I was so furious at the traitress, that I made up my

mind to leave Gibraltar without seeing her again. But at the first
roll of the drum, all my courage left me. I took my basket of
oranges and ran to Carmen's place. Her Venetian blind was
partly open, and I saw her big dark eyes watching me. The
powdered servant let me in at once. Carmen sent him on an
errand, and, as soon as we were alone, she went into one of her
silly outbursts of laughter and threw her arms around my neck.
I'd never seen her look so beautiful. Dressed up like a madonna,
perfumed . . . amid silken furniture and embroidered curtains
. . . Ah! . . . and me, dressed like the thief I was!

" *'Minchorrô,'* said Carmen, 'I feel like smashing up
everything here! I feel like setting fire to the house and running
away to the *sierra.*'[53]

"And there were caresses. . . and then laughter!. . . and she
danced, and she tore her ruffles. Never did a monkey leap more
wildly, make more grimaces, do more devilish tricks. When she
had again become serious, she said to me:

" 'Listen carefully! It's gypsy business. I want him to take
me to Ronda, where I have a sister who's a nun[54] . . . (Here new
bursts of laughter.) We'll pass by a spot that I'll indicate to you.
There you'll attack and rob him of everything. The best thing
would be to kill him as well, but. . . ,' she added with a diabolical
smile that she had at certain times (and that smile no one had any
desire to imitate!), . . . 'do you know what you should do? Let One
Eye come out first and lead the attack! You stay a little distance
behind him. The lobster is both brave and skillful, and he has
good pistols. . . Do you get my meaning?. . .'

"She interrupted herself with a new peal of laughter which
made me shudder.

" 'No,' I said to her, 'I hate García, but he's my comrade.
Perhaps one day I'll get rid of him for you, but we'll settle our
account the way we do it in my region. I'm a gypsy only by
chance, and, in certain matters, I'll always be a true Navarrese,
as the proverb says.'[55]

"She continued:

" 'You're a fool, a ninny, a real *payllo*! You're like the dwarf
who thought he was tall when he could spit a long way.[56] You
don't love me! Go away!'

"When she told me to go away, I couldn't go away. I promised to leave, to return to my comrades, and to lie in wait for the Englishman. On her part, she promised me to feign illness right up to the moment of leaving Gibraltar for Ronda. I stayed two more days at Gibraltar, and she even had the audacity to come disguised to see me at my inn. I left, and I too had my plan. I returned to our redezvous, knowing precisely the place and the time when the Englishman and Carmen would pass by. I found Dancaïre and García, who were waiting for me. We spent the night in a forest beside a fire of pine cones, which blazed marvelously. I suggested to García that we play a game of cards, and he accepted. In the second game, I told him that he was cheating, and he began to laugh. I threw the cards in his face. He tried to reach for his musket, but I put my foot on it and said to him: 'I'm told that you can handle a knife better than the cleverest rogue, in fact, like the champion of Málaga. Would you like to try your skill against me?'

"Dancaïre wanted to separate us. I had landed two or three punches on García. Anger made him brave, and he had pulled out his knife and I mine. Both of us told Dancaïre to give us room and let us fight it out. He saw that there was no way of stopping us, and so he stepped aside. García was already bent double, crouching like a cat ready to pounce upon a mouse. He was holding his hat in his left hand in order to parry, his knife thrust forward. That's their Andalusian guard. As for me, I took the Navarrese stance, right in front of him, my left arm raised, my left leg forward, my knife down along my right thigh. I felt stronger than a giant. Suddenly he leaped at me like a flash. I turned on my left foot, and he found nothing in front of him but air. But I struck him in the throat, and the knife went in so far that my hand was under his chin. I twisted the blade so hard that it broke. It was all over. The blade was forced out of the wound by a jet of blood as thick as your arm. He fell on his face as stiff as a board.

" 'What have you done?' Dancaïre said to me.

" 'Listen,' I said, 'we couldn't go on living together. I love Carmen, and I want to be the only one. Besides, García was a scoundrel, and I couldn't forget what he did to poor Remendado.

There's only two of us now, but we're good fellows. Come, do you want me as your sworn friend for life?'

"Dancaïre extended his hand to me. He was a man of fifty.

" 'To the devil with love affairs!' he exclaimed. 'If you'd asked him for Carmen, he'd have sold her to you for a piastre. With only two of us left now, how will we manage it tomorrow?'

" 'Let me do it all be myself,' I replied. 'Now I can take on the whole world.'

"We buried García and then pitched our camp two hundred paces away. The next day, Carmen and her Englishman came along with two muleteers and a servant. I said to Dancaïre:

" 'I'll take care of the Englishman. You frighten away the others; they are not armed.'

"The Englishman had courage. If Carmen hadn't pushed his arm, he'd have killed me. In short, that day I won Carmen back, and my first words to her were to tell her that she was now a widow. When she found out from me how that had happened, she said:

" 'You'll always be a *lillipendi*! García should have killed you. Your Navarrese style is just a big joke, and he's killed much better fighters than you. It happened because his time had come. Yours will come too!'

" 'And yours,' I replied, 'if you're not a faithful *romi* to me.'

" 'All right,' she said, 'I've seen it more than once in the coffee grounds that we'd end up together. Bah! What must be, must be!'

"And she clacked her castanets, as she always did when she wanted to banish some bothersome idea.

"A man forgets when he's talking about himself. All these details are, no doubt, boring you, but I'll soon be finished. The life we were leading lasted for quite some time. Dancaïre and I gathered around us some fellows who were more reliable than the original band, and we were kept busy with our smuggling. Sometimes, too, I must admit, we staged holdups on the highway, but only as a last resort and when we couldn't do otherwise. Besides, we didn't mistreat the travellers, and we confined ourselves to stealing their money.

"For some months I was happy with Carmen. She continued to be useful to us in our operations by notifying us of good hauls that we could make. She stayed in Málaga, or in Cordova, or in Granada, but in response to a word from me, she would leave everything and come to join me at an isolated *venta* or even in camp. Only once, in Málaga, did she cause me some worry. I found out that she'd made a very rich merchant her target, and that she was probably preparing to start her Gibraltar tricks all over again with him. In spite of everything that Dancaïre could say to stop me, I left, and I entered Málaga in broad daylight. I sought out Carmen and brought her back at once. We had a fierce quarrel.

" 'Do you know what,' she said to me, 'since you've been my *rom* for keeps, I love you less than when you were my *minchorrô*? I don't want to be pestered, and especially I don't want to be ordered about. What I want is to be free and to do what I please. Take care not to push me to the limit. If you bore me, I'll find some fine fellow, who'll do to you what you did to One Eye.'

"Dancaïre patched things up between us, but we had said things to each other which rankled in our hearts. We no longer felt the same toward each other as before. Soon after that, bad luck struck us. The military attacked us by surprise. Dancaïre was killed, as well as two of my comrades. Two others were captured. As for me, I was seriously wounded, and but for my good horse I'd have fallen into the hands of the soldiers. Utterly exhausted, and with a bullet in my body, I went to hide in a wood with the only comrade left to me. I fainted as I was getting off my horse, and I thought I was going to die in the underbrush like a rabbit which has been shot full of lead. My comrade carried me into a cave we knew; then he went to get Carmen. She was in Granada, and she hastened to me at once.

"For two weeks she didn't leave me for an instant. She didn't shut an eye all that time. She nursed me with a skill and devotion such as no woman has ever shown for the most loved of men! As soon as I was able to stand on my legs again, she took me to Granada with the greatest secrecy. Gypsy women find safe shelter everywhere, and I spent more than six weeks in a house which was two doors away from the magistrate who was looking for me. More than once, looking out from behind the shutters, I saw him pass by. At last I felt well again, but I had done a good deal of thinking on my bed of pain, and I made up my mind to change my life. I spoke to Carmen about leaving Spain and trying to live honestly in the New World. She laughed at me.

" 'We're not made for planting cabbages,' she said, 'our destiny in life, yours and mine, is to live at the expense of the *payllos*. Listen, I've made a dèal, with Nathan ben-Joseph of Gibraltar. He's got some cotton fabrics which are just lying there waiting for you to smuggle them in. He knows that you're alive, and he's counting on you. What would our correspondents in Gibraltar say, if you didn't keep your word to them?'

"I let myself be inveigled, and I again took up my sordid trade.

"While I was hiding out in Granada, there were bullfights which Carmen attended. When she came home, she talked a great deal about a very skillful picador named Lucas. She knew the name of his horse, and how much his embroidered vest had cost him. I paid no attention to it at the time. Then, some days later, Juanito, my sole remaining comrade, told me that he'd seen Carmen with Lucas at a store in the Zacatín. That began to alarm me. I asked Carmen how and why she had become acquainted with the picador.

" 'He's a young fellow,' she said, 'with whom we can do business. A noisy stream must have in it either water or pebbles.[57] He's won twelve hundred *reals* in the bullfights. We must do one of two things: either we must get this money, or, since he's a good horseman and a plucky fellow, we can take him into our band. So-and-so and so-and-so are dead; you need to replace them. Take him with you.'

" 'I don't want either his money or him personally,' I replied, 'and I forbid you to talk to him again.'

" 'Beware!' she said. 'When anyone defies me to do something, I do it right away!'

"Fortunately, the picador left for Málaga, and I for my part made my preparations to smuggle in the Jew's cotton fabrics. I had a great deal to do on this expedition and Carmen did too. I forgot all about Lucas and perhaps she also forgot him, for the moment at least.

"It was just about that time, sir, that I met you, first near Montilla, then later at Cordova. I won't talk about our last interview. Perhaps you know more about it than I do. Carmen stole your watch; she also wanted your money and especially that ring which I see on your finger. She said it was a magic ring and that it was very important for her to possess it. We had a violent quarrel, and I struck her. She grew pale and wept. It was the first time that I'd ever seen her cry, and it made me feel terrible. I begged her to forgive me, but she sulked for a whole day, and, when I left for Montilla, she wouldn't kiss me. My heart was heavy, but, three days later, she came to join me with a smile on her face and as gay as a lark. Everything was forgotten, and we looked like a pair of newly-met lovers. When it was time to part, she said to me:

" 'There's a fiesta in Cordova. I'm going there, for then I'll find out which people will be going away with money, and I'll tell you.'

"I let her go. When I was alone, I thought about the fiesta and the change of mood on the part of Carmen. 'It must be that she's already had her revenge,' I said to myself, 'since she's come back to me first to make up.' A peasant told me that there was bullfighting at Cordova. Then my blood began to boil, and, like a madman, I left and went straight to the bull ring. Lucas was pointed out to me, and, on the bench next to the barrier, I recognized Carmen. A moment's glance at her was enough to make my suspicion a certainty. When the first bull came into the ring, Lucas—as I had expected—became a real gallant. He snatched the cockade[58] off the bull and presented it to Carmen, who promptly put it in her hair. The bull then took it upon himself to avenge me. Lucas was knocked down with his horse on his chest, and the bull on top of both of them. I looked at the place where Carmen was sitting, but she wasn't there any more. It was impossible for me to leave my seat, so I had to wait until the bullfights were at an end. Then I went to the house which you already know, and I bided my time there the whole evening and during a part of the night. About two o'clock in the morning, Carmen returned and was somewhat surprised to see me.

" 'Come with me,' I said.

" 'Very well,' she answered, 'let's go!'

"I went to get my horse and put her up behind me. We rode all the rest of the night without saying a word to each other. At dawn, we stopped at an isolated *venta*, quite close to a little hermitage. There I said to Carmen:

" 'Listen to me! I'll forget everything. I won't mention anything about it again, but swear one thing to me: that you'll come with me to America, and that you'll live a respectable life there.'

" 'No,' she said in a sulky tone, 'I won't go to America. I like it here.'

" 'That's because you're near Lucas,' I replied. 'But think it over. Even if he recovers, he'll never make old bones. Besides, why should I bear a grudge against him? I'm tired of killing all your lovers. You're the one I'll kill the next time.'

"She looked at me with a fixed stare in her wild eyes, and then she said to me:

" 'I've always thought you'd kill me. The very first time you saw me, I'd just met a priest at the door of my house. And tonight, as we were leaving Cordova, didn't you notice anything? A rabbit ran across the road between your horse's feet. That is fate!'

" 'Carmencita,' I said, 'don't you love me any more?'

"She didn't answer. She was sitting cross-legged on a reed mat, tracing lines on the ground with her finger.

" 'Let's change our way of life, Carmen,' I said to her in a pleading tone. 'Let's go away and live some place where we'll never be separated. You know that we've got a hundred and twenty ounces of gold buried under an oak not far from here. Besides, we have some additional funds at the house of Nathan ben-Joseph the Jew.'

"She began to smile, and then she said to me:

" 'First me, then you. I know that it must happen that way.'

" 'Think it over,' I continued, 'I'm at the end of my patience and my courage. Make up your mind, or else I'll make up mine.'

"I left her and went for a walk in the direction of the hermitage. I found the hermit absorbed in prayer. I waited until his prayer was at an end. I too would have liked to pray, but I couldn't. When he was no longer kneeling, I went over to him.

" 'Father,' I said, 'will you pray for someone who is in grave danger?'

" 'I pray for all who are afflicted,' he replied.

" 'Can you say a Mass for a soul which is perhaps going to appear before its Maker?' I asked.

" 'Yes,' he answered, looking hard at me with a fixed stare, and, as there was something strange in my appearance, he tried to make me talk.

" 'It seems to me that I've seen you before,' he said.

"I put a piastre on his bench.

" 'When will you be saying the Mass?' I asked him.

" 'In half an hour. The son of the innkeeper over yonder will come to serve it. But tell me, young man, haven't you something on your conscience which is troubling you? Will you listen to the advice of a Christian?'

"I felt close to tears. I told him that I would come back, and I ran out of the hermitage. I lay down on the grass until I heard the bell. Then I went back to the chapel, but I remained outside. When the Mass was over, I returned to the *venta*. I hoped that Carmen had fled; she could have taken my horse and ridden away... but I found her there still. She didn't want it to be said that I had frightened her. During my absence, she had unstitched the hem of her dress in order to take out the lead that weighed it down. Now she was sitting before a table looking into a bowl of water at the lead which she had melted and dropped into it. She was so absorbed in her magic that at first she didn't notice that I had returned. First she'd take a piece of lead out of the bowl and turn it around on all sides with a sad look on her face; then she'd sing one of those magic songs in which gypsy women conjure up María Padilla, mistress of Don Pedro, who was said to be the *Bari Crallisa,* or the Grand Queen of the Gypsies.[59]

" 'Carmen,' I said to her, 'will you come with me?'

"She stood up, threw aside her wooden bowl, and put her mantilla over her head, ready to leave. My horse was led up, she mounted behind me, and we rode away.

" 'Well, Carmen,' I said to her, after we had travelled a stretch of the road, 'you're willing to follow me now, aren't you?'

" 'Yes,' she replied, 'I'll follow you even unto death, but I'll no longer live with you.'

"We were in a lonely gorge. I stopped my horse.

" 'Is this the place?' she asked.

"With one leap she was on the ground. She took off her mantilla, threw it at her feet, and stood motionless looking at me with a fixed stare, one hand on her hip.

" 'You intend to kill me, I'm quite aware of that,' she said, 'it's fate. But you'll never make me yield.'

" 'I beg you,' I pleaded with her, 'be reasonable. Listen to me! All the past is forgotten. You know, of course, that you're the one who's ruined me, that it's all because of you that I've become a bandit and a murderer. Carmen, my Carmen! Let me save you and myself with you!'

" 'José,' she replied, 'what you're asking me to do is impossible. I don't love you any more. You still love me, and that's why you want to kill me. I could easily tell you another lie, if I wished, but I don't want to bother to do so. It's over between us. As my *rom* you've the right to kill me, your *romi,* but Carmen will always be free! A *calli* she was born, and a *calli* she will die.'

" 'Then you love Lucas?' I asked her.

" 'Yes, I've loved him, as I've loved you, for a little while, less than I've loved you perhaps. Right now I love nothing any more, and I hate myself for having loved you.'

"I threw myself down at her feet. I took hold of her hands, and I wet them with my tears. I reminded her of all the happy moments we had spent together. I offered to remain a bandit just to please her. Everything, sir, everything—I offered her everything, if only she would love me again!

"To my pleading she replied:

" 'Love you again? That's impossible. Live with you? I won't do it!'

"A wild rage took possession of me. I drew out my knife. I would have liked her to look afraid and beg me for mercy, but that woman was a devil.

" 'For the last time,' I shouted, 'will you live with me?'

" 'No! No! No!' she said, stamping her foot.

"And she pulled a ring which I'd given her off her finger, and threw it into the underbrush.

"I stabbed her twice. It was One Eye's knife, which I'd taken from him because I had broken my own. At the second blow she fell without a whimper. I think that I can still see her big black eyes looking at me in a fixed stare. Then they became clouded and closed. For a good hour, I remained prostrate with grief before her corpse. Then I remembered that Carmen had often told me that she'd like to be buried in a wood. I dug a grave for her with my knife, and I laid her in it. I searched a long time for her ring, and at last I found it. I placed it in the grave beside her, with a little cross. Perhaps I was wrong. Then I mounted my horse, galloped to Cordova, and at the first guardhouse I turned myself in. I said that I had killed Carmen, but I wouldn't tell where her body was. The hermit was a holy man. He prayed for her. He said a Mass for her soul. Poor child! It is the gypsies who are to blame for having brought her up that way!''

Carmen – IV

Spain is one of the countries in which those nomads, scattered all over Europe and known as *Bohemians, Gitanos, Gypsies, Zigeuner,* and so forth, are still to be found in the greatest numbers. The majority live, or rather lead a vagabond life, in the provinces of the south and of the east, in Andalusia, in Estramadura, and in the realm of Murcia. There are also a great many of them in Catalonia. The latter often cross over into France, and one encounters them at all our fairs in the south of France. Usually the men practice the trades of horse dealer,

veterinarian, and mule shearer. To these they add the trade of
mending pans and copper utensils, not to mention smuggling
and other illegal practices. The women tell fortunes, beg, and sell
all sorts of drugs, harmless or otherwise.

The physical characteristics of the gypsies are easier to
distinguish than to describe, and when you have seen just one of
them you can recognize an individual of that race out of a
thousand other men. It is their physiognomy and their facial
expression, especially, which make them different from the other
inhabitants of the same country. Their complexion is very
swarthy, always darker than that of the people among whom they
live. This is the reason for the name *calé*, the black ones, which
they often use to describe themselves.[60] Their eyes are
decidedly slanted, deep set, very dark, and shaded by long, thick
lashes. Their gaze can be compared only to that of a wild deer.
Boldness and timidity are etched in it at the same time, and in
that respect their eyes reveal very well the character of their race:
cunning and bold, but with "a natural fear of blows," like
Panurge.[61] The men are, for the most part, well built, slim and
agile. I do not believe that I have ever seen a gypsy with a paunch.

In Germany, the gypsy women are often very pretty, but
beauty is very rare among the Spanish *gitanas*. When they are
very young, they may pass as attractive ugly ducklings, but once
they have reached motherhood, they become positively
repulsive. The filthiness of both sexes is unbelievable, and
anyone who has not seen a mature gypsy woman's hair will find it
difficult to imagine just what it is like, even if he conjures up the
coarsest, the greasiest, the dustiest horse hair possible. In some
of the big cities of Andalusia, some young gypsy girls who are
somewhat prettier than the others take better care of their
personal appearance. These girls, for money, perform dances
which greatly resemble those we prohibit at our public balls at
carnival time. Mr. Borrow, an English missionary and author of
two very interesting works on the Spanish gypsies, whom he
undertook to convert on behalf of the Bible Society, declares that
there is no example on record of any *gitana* ever showing the
slightest partiality for a man foreign to her race.

It seems to me that there is a great deal of exaggeration in the tributes he pays to their chastity. In the first place, the great majority find themselves in the same situation as the ugly woman referred to by Ovid: *Casta quam nemo rogavit.*[62] As for the pretty ones, they are like all Spanish girls, fussy in the choice of their lovers. A man must take their fancy, must merit their favors. Mr. Borrow cites as proof of their virtue a trait which does honor to his own, especially to his *naïveté*. He states that an immoral man; a man of his acquaintance, once offered several ounces of gold to a pretty *gitana,* but all in vain. An Andalusian to whom I told this anecdote claimed that the immoral man in question would have had much more success if he had offered her two or three *piastres,* He assured me that an offer of several ounces of gold to a gypsy girl was as bad a way of trying to persuade her as to promise a million or two to a chambermaid at an inn.

However that may be, it is certain that the *gitanas* show an extraordinary devotion to their husbands. There is no danger or discomfort they will not endure in order to help them in their need. One of the names which the gypsies give themselves, *romè* or "the married people," seems to me to attest to the respect of their race for the state of matrimony. Generally speaking, it may be said that their chief virtue is their patriotism, if that is what the loyalty may be called which they observe in their relations with individuals of the same origin as themselves, their eagerness to help one another, and the inviolable secrecy they keep for each other in compromising circumstances. For that matter, in all mysterious associations beyond the pale of the law, something similar may be observed.

Some months ago, I paid a visit to a band of gypsies who had settled in the Vosges. In the hut of an old woman, the eldest of her tribe, there was a gypsy man, a stranger to her family, who was stricken with a mortal illness. This man had left a hospital, where he was being well cared for, so that he might die among his own countrymen. For thirteen weeks he had been bedridden in the hut of his hosts and had received much better treatment than the sons and sons-in-law who were living in the same house. He had a good bed, made of straw and moss, with sheets which were tolerably white, whereas the rest of the family, numbering eleven persons, slept on planks which were three feet long. So much for their hospitality. This same woman, who was so humane toward her guest, said to me in front of the sick man, *"Singo, singo, homte hi mulo:* soon, soon he must die." After all, the lives of these people are so miserable, that the approach of death holds no terror for them.

One remarkabe trait in the gypsies' character is their indifference in matters of religion. It is not that they are freethinkers or skeptics, nor have they ever made any profession of atheism—far from it. The religion of the land they inhabit is theirs too, but they change it when they change countries. The superstitions which replace religious sentiment in the minds of uncultured peoples, are equally foreign to them. Indeed, how can superstition exist among people who most of the time live on the credulity of others? I've noticed, however, that the Spanish gypsies have a singular horror of coming into contact with a corpse. There are few of them who would consent, even for money, to carry a dead body to the cemetery.

I have said that most gypsy women dabble in fortune telling. They do this extremely well. But for them something which is the. source of great profit is the sale of charms and love potions. Not only do they keep a supply of toads' feet to steady fickle hearts, or filings of lodestone to kindle love for oneself in indifferent lovers, but also, if need be, they pronounce powerful incantations which compel the Devil to lend them his help. Last year, a Spanish lady told me the following story. One day she was walking along Alcalá Street, very sad and preoccupied. A gypsy woman who was squatting on the sidewalk called to her: "Pretty lady, your lover has betrayed you." (It was the truth.) "Do you want me to make him come back to you?" One can easily understand with what great joy this proposal was accepted, and how great must have been the confidence inspired by a person who could guess at a glance the innermost secrets of the heart.

As it would have been impossible to proceed with the performance of the magic operations in the most crowded street in Madrid, they agreed on a meeting place for the next day. "Nothing will be easier than to bring back the unfaithful one to your feet," said the *gitana*. "Do you by any chance happen to have a handkerchief, a scarf, or a mantilla on you that he has given you?" She gave the gypsy a silk neckerchief. "Now sew a *piastre* in one corner of the neckerchief with scarlet silk thread. In another corner sew a half *piastre*. Here sew a small coin, and there a two-*real* piece. Then, in the center, you must sew a gold piece—a doubloon would be best." The doubloon and the other coins were sewn in. "Now give me the kerchief. I'm going to take it to the Campo Santo [63] at the stroke of midnight. Come with me, if you'd like to see a fine bit of witchcraft. I promise you that no later than tomorrow you will see again the one you love." The gypsy woman set off for the Campo Santo alone, for the lady was too much afraid of devils to accompany her. I leave it to you to decide whether or not the poor forsaken lady ever saw her kerchief or her unfaithful lover again.

In spite of their poverty and a sort of aversion that they inspire, the gypsies do, nevertheless, enjoy a certain consideration and recognition among uneducated people, and they are very proud of it. They consider themselves to be a superior race as far as intelligence is concerned, and heartily despise the people whose hospitality they enjoy. "The Gentiles are so stupid," a gypsy woman of the Vosges told me, "that there's no merit in making fools of them. The other day a peasant woman called out to me in the street. I went into her house. Her stove was smoking, and she asked me to cast a spell to make it burn properly. First of all, I made her give me a good piece of bacon. Then I began to mumble some words in Romany. 'You're a fool,' I said, 'you were born a fool, and you'll die a fool. . .' When I was near the door, I said to her in good German: 'The surest way to stop your stove from smoking is not to light a fire in it.' And I took to my heels."

The history of the gypsies is still a puzzle. It is known for a fact that their first bands, which were very few in number, appeared in Eastern Europe toward the beginning of the fifteenth century. But no one can say where they came from, or why they came to Europe. What is even more extraordinary is that nobody knows how they multiplied in a short period of time in so prodigious a fashion in several countries far removed from one another. The gypsies themselves have preserved no tradition regarding their origin, and if the majority of them speak of Egypt as their original homeland, it is because they have accepted a tale circulated a very long time ago about their race.

Most Orientalists who have studied the gypsy language believe that they originated in India. In fact, it would appear that a large number of roots and many grammatical forms in Romany are to be found in idioms derived from the Sanskrit. As may be imagined, in their long peregrinations the gypsies have adopted many foreign words. In every Romany dialect, a number of Greek words are to be found. For example, *cocal*, bone, from κόκκαλον; *petalli*, horseshoe, from πέταλον; cafi, nail, from καρφί, etc.

Today the gypsies have almost as many different dialects as there are separate tribes of their race. Everywhere they speak the language of the country they inhabit more easily than their own idiom, which they seldom use except to be able to converse freely before strangers. If the dialect of the German gypsies is compared with that of the Spanish gypsies, who have had no communication with the former for centuries, a very large number of common words can be recognized. But everywhere, the original language has noticeably changed, although in different degrees, by contact with the more cultivated languages which these nomads have been obliged to use. German on the one hand, and Spanish on the other, have so modified the basic Romany tongue that it would be impossible for a gypsy of the Black Forest to converse with one of his Andalusian brothers, even though the exchange of a few sentences would suffice for them to recognize that each is speaking a dialect derived from the same language. Some words in very frequent use are, I believe, common to all dialects. Thus, in all the vocabularies which I have had an opportunity to consult *pani* means water; *manro,* bread; *mâs,* meat; and *lon,* salt.

The words for numbers are almost the same everywhere.

The German dialect seems to me to be much purer than the Spanish dialect, for it has preserved a number of primitive grammatical forms, whereas the *gitanos* of Spain have adopted those of Castilian Spanish. Yet some words constitute an exception, attesting to the fact that there was an ancient language community and a common tongue. The preterites of the German dialect are formed by adding -*ium* to the imperative, which is always the root of the verb. In the Spanish Romany dialect, the verbs are all conjugated on the model of the first conjugation of Castilian verbs. From the infinitive *jamar*, to eat, the regularly derived form should be *jamé*, I have eaten; from *lillar*, to take, it should be *lillé*, I have taken. Some old gypsies, however, say *jayon, lillon*, by way of exception. I know of no other verbs which have preserved this ancient form.

While I am thus displaying my meager knowledge of the Romany language, I should point out some French slang words which our thieves have borrowed from the gypsies. *Les Mystères de Paris* have taught honest folks that *chourin* means knife. This is a pure Romany word, *tchouri* being one of the words which is common to all gypsy dialects. Monsieur Vidocq calls a horse *grès*, which is again a gypsy word: *gras, gre, graste, gris*. Add to this the word *romanichel*, which, in Parisian slang, means the gypsies. It is a corruption of *romané tchavé*, gypsy fellows. But one derivation of my own, of which I am very proud, is the one for the word *frimousse*, facial expression, face, features, a word that every school child uses, or at least did use in my day. In the first place, it should be noted that Oudin, in his curious dictionary published in 1640, wrote *firmilouse*. Now, in Romany *firla* or *fila* means face, features, and *mui* has the same meaning, for it is precisely the *os* of the Latins. The combination *firlamui* was immediately understood by a gypsy purist, and I believe it to be true to the spirit of his language.

But that is quite enough to give the readers of *Carmen* a favorable idea of my studies about Romany. I shall conclude my tale with this proverb, which I believe to be very fitting here: *En retudi panda nasti abela macha:* into a closed mouth no fly can enter.[64]

Notes on the Translation

[1] These words have been left by Mérimée in the original Greek, with no translation. In English they mean: "Woman is as bitter as bile; there are, however, two circumstances when she is pleasant: in bed, and when she is dead."

[2] *Bellum Hispaniense*: *The Spanish War*, written by an anonymous author.

[3] *Commentaries*: These are the well-known *Commentaries* by Julius Caesar, dealing with his great military campaigns against the various barbarian tribes in Western Europe, including Spain. As has already been indicated (page 29), the Frenchman who narrates the story is carrying with him a copy of Caesar's *Commentaries* and a few shirts as his only baggage. The word *Elzévir* refers to a book printed by the Elzevirs, publishers in Amsterdam (1592-1681), who were celebrated for their fine editions of the classics, usually in small volumes. Mérimée uses the term again in his *Colomba*, Chapter XX: *Vous aurez un Elzévir, Monsieur*, "You shall have an Elzevir, sir," that is, a fine Elzevir edition.

[4] In the *Bible*, Book of Judges 8:5-6, it is stated that Gideon rejected soldiers who drank straight from a stream instead of scooping up water with their hands and watching for the enemy at the same time.

[5] The Andalusians aspirate the *s* and confuse it with the soft *c* and the *z*, which the Castilians pronounce like the English *th*. An

Andalusian can be recognized by the word *señor* alone (Mérimée's note).

6 *The privileged provinces,* which enjoy special *fueros,* that is, Alava, Biscay, Guipuzcoa and part of Navarre. Basque is the language of the region (Mérimée's note).

7 Actaeon: a celebrated huntsman, saw Diana with her nymphs bathing, whereupon the goddess changed him into a stag, in which form he was torn to pieces by his own dogs.

8 A *café* which has an ice chest, or rather an icehouse. In Spain there is scarcely a single village without its *nevería* (Mérimée's note).

9 In Spain, every traveller who is not carrying around with him some samples of calico or silk is assumed to be an Englishman, an *inglesito.* It is the same in the East. In Chalcis I have had the honor of being introduced as a Μιλόρδος Φραντζέσος. (Mérimée's note). The Greek words mean French milord.

10 Your fortune (Mérimée's note).

11 In 1830, the nobility still enjoyed this privilege. Today, under the constitutional regime, commoners have won the right to the *garrote* (Mérimée's note).

12 Basque iron-tipped staves (Mérimée's note).

13 The regular attire of girls in Navarre and the other Basque provinces (Mérimée's note).

14 *Isn't a broom good enough for you?* : Carmen is implying that the other woman is a witch.

15 *Pintar un javeque:* to paint a sailboat. Spanish sailboats

usually have their sides painted with red and white squares (Mérimée's note). The reference is to the X which Carmen slashes on her adversary's cheek.

16 Yes, sir (Mérimée's note).

17 *I'd like to have a father confessor from the Provinces:* This refers, of course, to Don José's present predicament, awaiting execution. See note 6 regarding *the privileged provinces.*

18 Plot of land, garden (Mérimée's note).

19 Toughs, braggarts (Mérimée's note).

20 The entire Spanish cavalry is armed with lances (Mérimée's note).

21 Alcalá de los Panaderos is a village two leagues from Seville, where delicious bread and rolls are made. It is claimed that they owe their quality to the water of Alcalá. Large quantities of them are brought into Seville every day (Mérimée's note).

22 Good day, comrade (Mérimée's note).

23 Most houses in Seville have an inner courtyard surrounded by porticos. It is used as a sitting room in the summertime. This courtyard is covered by an awning which is sprinkled with water during the day, and removed in the evening. The street door is almost always open, and the passage leading to the courtyard, the *zaguán,* is barred by an elegantly wrought iron gate (Mérimée's note).

24 *Mañana será otro día.* Spanish proverb (Mérimée's note).

25 *Chuquel sos pirela, cocal terela.* Gypsy proverb (Mérimée's note). The words mean: A dog that wanders finds a bone.

26 Sugared yolks of eggs (Mérimée's note).

27 A sort of nougat (Mérimée's note).

28 King Don Pedro, whom we call *The Cruel* and whom Queen Isabella the Catholic always called *The Just,* loved to roam the streets of Seville at night in search of adventures, like Caliph Haroun-al-Raschid. One night in a lonely street he picked a quarrel with a man who was playing a serenade. There was a fight, and the king killed the amorous cavalier. Hearing the sound of the swords, an old woman put her head out of the window and lighted up the scene with the small lamp, *candilejo,* that she was holding in her hand. It should be noted that King Don Pedro, though strong and agile, had a strange physical peculiarity. When he walked, his kneecaps made a loud, cracking noise. The old woman had no difficulty in recognizing him by this cracking. The next day the magistrate on duty came to make his report to the king:

> "Sire, there was a duel last night in such and such
> a street. One of the combatants was killed."
> "Have you discovered who the murderer was?"
> "Yes, Sire."
> "Why has he not been punished as yet?"
> "Sire, I await your orders."
> "Carry out the law."

Now the king had just issued a decree to the effect that any duellist was to be beheaded, and that his head was to be displayed at the site of the duel. The magistrate got out of the difficulty by using his wits. He had the head of a statue of the king sawed off and displayed in a niche in the middle of the block where the killing had occurred. The king and all the inhabitants of Seville thought this very good. The street took its name from the lamp of the old woman who was the sole witness to the affair. This is the popular tradition. Zúñiga gives a slightly different version. (See *Anales de Sevilla,* vol. II, p. 136.) Be that as it may, there is still a Candilejo Street in Seville, and in that street a stone bust said to be a likeness of Don Pedro. Unfortunately, this bust is modern; the old one was very weather-beaten in the seventeenth century, and the city council at that time had it replaced by the one which can be seen today (Mérimée's note).

29 *Romany*: the name given to the gypsy language.

30 *Rom*: husband; *romi*: wife (Mérimée's note).

31 *Calo*, feminine; *calli*, plural; *cales*: (literally) *black*, the name that the gypsies apply to themselves in their own language (Mérimée's note).

32 *The romalis:* the lively gypsy dance performed by Carmen here and previously at the colonel's party.

33 Spanish dragoons are dressed in yellow (Mérimée's note).

34 *A dog and a wolf don't make a good household for long*: a common Spanish proverb.

35 *Me dicas vriardâ de jorpoy, bus ne sino braco*. Gypsy proverb (Mérimée's note). In the preceding sentence Carmen also alludes to a common medieval proverb: *The devil is not always as black as he is painted.*

36 The Holy Virgin (Mérimée's note).

37 The scaffold, which is the widow of the man last hanged on it (Mérimée's note).

38 The red (land) (Mérimée's note).

39 There is a play on words here by Mérimée. In French, *dragon* means both "dragon" and "dragoon."

40 *Flamenca de Roma*: a slang term for gypsy women. Here, *Roma* does not mean the Eternal City, but the race of the Romi or *married people*, the name gypsies give themselves. The first gypsies seen in Spain probably came from the Low Countries, hence their name: *Flemings* (Mérimée's note).

[41] *Chufas:* a bulbous root out of which a rather delicious drink is made (Mérimée's note).

[42] *Chippe calli:* the gypsy language (also called *rommani* or *Romany*).

[43] The staple diet of a Spanish soldier (Mérimée's note).

[44] *Ustilar a pastesas,* to steal cleverly, to steal without violence (Mérimée's note).

[45] *Miñons:* A kind of volunteer militia (Mérimée's note).

[46] *Sarapia sat pesquital ne punzava* (Mérimée's note).

[47] Vejer and Tarifa are southern coastal towns near the Strait of Gibraltar.

[48] Ah! What idiots! They take me for a lady (Mérimée's note)!

[49] The name the Spanish give to the English because of the color of their uniforms (Mérimée's note).

[50] *Ad finibus terrae*: to prison, or to the Devil (Mérimée's note).

[51] *Minchorrô*: my lover, or rather, my fancy (Mérimée's note).

[52] *Maquila*: an iron-tipped Basque staff; see also note 12.

[53] *Sierra*: this Spanish word means literally a *saw*; but it has also the figurative meaning of a *mountain*, as in the names *la Sierra de Ronda* and *la Sierra de Gaucin* in this story.

[54] *I want him to take me to Ronda, where I have a sister who is a nun*: is what Carmen has told the English lord. It is, of course a trap.

55 *Navarro fino* (Mérimée's note).

56 *Or esorjlé de or narsichislé, sin chismar lachinguel.* Gypsy proverb. Prowess for a dwarf is to spit a long way (Mérimée's note).

57 Len sos sonsi abela Pani o reblendani terela (Gypsy proverb, Mérimée's note).

58 *Cockade:* (*la divisa*) is a knot of ribbons, indicating by its color the farm from which the bull comes. It is fastened to the bull's hide by means of a hook, and it is the height of gallantry to snatch it off the living animal and offer it to a woman (Mérimée's note).

59 Maria Padilla is said to have bewitched King Don Pedro. A popular legend relates that she had given the queen, Blanche de Bourbon, a golden girdle which to the eyes of the bewitched king looked like a live snake. From this came the repugnance he always showed toward the unfortunate queen (Mérimée's note). In the text, Mérimée also refers to Maria Padilla as the *Bari Crallisa*, that is, the Grand Queen of the Gypsies.

60 It seems to me that the German gypsies, although they understand perfectly the word *Calé*, do not like to be known by it. They call themselves *Romané tchavé* (Mérimée's note).

61 *Panurge*: a character in Rabelais' *Pantagruel* who has "a natural fear of blows" as his outstanding characteristic.

62 *Casta quam nemo rogavit*: *Chaste is she whom no one has asked.*

63 The Campo Santo is the cemetery.

64 The Spaniards have the same proverb: *En boca cerrada no entran moscas.*

Chronology
of Prosper Mérimée's Works

TITLE	DATE OF PUBLICATION
Report Made to the Society for the Encouragement of National Industry, in the Name of the Committee of Chemical Arts, on some Prussian Blue Samples	1821
Theatre of Clara Gazul, Spanish Commedienne, by Joseph L'Estrange	1825
Historical Notice on the Life and Works of Cervantes (Prefixed to a translation by Monsieur Filleau de St. Martin)	1826
La Guzla, or Choice of Illyric Poetry, collected in Dalmatia, Bosnia, Croatia, and Herzegovinia	1827
The Jacquerie, Feudal Scenes, followed by The Cavajal Family, a Drama	1828
Chronicle of the Reign of Charles IX	1829
The Double Blunder	1833
Mosaic (Colleciton of Tales and Novellas): The Fiacre of the Holy Sacrament (1829); Mateo Falcone (1829); Vision of Charles XI (1829); The Taking of the Redoubt (1829); Tamango (1829); The Pearl of Toledo (1830); The Tric-Trac Party (1830); The Etruscan Vase (1830); The Malcontents (1830); Letters from Spain (1830)	1833
Notes on a Voyage in the South of France	1835
Notes on a Voyage in the West of France	1836
Notes on a Voyage in Auvergne and Limousin	1838
Notes on a Voyage in Corsica	1840
Colomba	1840
Essay on the Social War	1841
Essay on the Social War (1841); followed by The Venus of Ille (1837); Souls in Purgatory (1837); and Mosaic (1833)	1842

Posthumous Publications

Bibliography

Albert, Paul. "Prosper Mérimée, sa carrière et son art." In *La Littérature française du dix-neuvième siècle*, pp. 298-308. Paris: Perrin, 1925.

Beyle, Marie Henri [Stendhal]. *Prosper Mérimée*. Paris: Desoer, n.d.

Daudy, Philippe. *Prosper Mérimée*. Paris: Ditis, 1964.

D'Haussonville, Othenin. "Prosper Mérimée, à propos de ses lettres inédites." *La Revue des Deux-Mondes* 4 (1879): 21-39.

De Bury, H. Blaze. Avant-propos aux *Lettres à une autre inconnue*, par Prosper Mérimée. Paris: Amyot, 1881.

Du Bos, Charles. "Réflexions sur Prosper Mérimée." In *Approximations*, pp. 509-563. Paris: Hachette, 1949.

Faguet, Émile. "Prosper Mérimée." In *Le dix-neuvième siècle: études littéraires*, pp. 235-251. Paris: Société française d'imprimerie et de librairie, 1889.

Falcke, Ernst. "Die romantischen Elemente in Prosper Mérimées Romane und Novellen." *Romantische Arbeiten* 6 (1915): 12-33. (Leipzig)

Filon, Augustin. "Prosper Mérimée, d'après des souvenirs personnels et des documents inédits." *La Revue des Deux-Mondes* 18 (1893): 11-29.

————. *Prosper Mérimée et ses amis*. Paris: Amyot, 1894.

Gosse, Edmund. *The Life of Prosper Mérimée*. London: Heinemann, 1910.

Henriot, Émile. "Prosper Mérimée." In *Les Maîtres de la Littérature française*, pp. 87-101. Paris: Audin, 1932.

James, Henry. "Mérimée's Letters." In *French Poets and Novelists*. London: Macmillan, 1897.

Jovanovic, V.M. *La Guzla de Prosper Mérimée; étude d'histoire romantique*. Paris: Charpentier, 1911.

King, Grace. "Biographical and Critical Sketch of Prosper Mérimée." In *Library of the World's Best Literature*, pp. 9941-9955. New York: Schirmer, n.d.

Lemaître, Jules. "Prosper Mérimée." In *Les Contemporains*. Paris: Garnier, 1877.

Lion, Henri. "Prosper Mérimée." In *Pages choisies des grands écrivains.* Paris: Didier, 1906.

Pailleron, M.L. "Prosper Mérimée." *La Revue des Deux-Mondes* 22 (1897): 37-55.

Parturier, Maurice. *Lettres de Prosper Mérimée à Madame de Beaulaincourt, 1866-1870.* Paris: Calman-Lévy, 1936.

Peter, Walter. "Prosper Mérimée." In *Studies in European Literature, Taylorian Lectures, 1889-1899.* London; Macmillan, 1900.

Pinvert, L. *Sur Prosper Mérimée: notes bibliographiques et critiques.* Paris: Didot, 1908.

Pritchett, V.S. "Prosper Mérimée." In *The Living Novel,* pp. 207-212. London: Routledge, 1946.

————. "Prosper Mérimée." In *The Living Novel and Later Appreciations,* pp. 347-353. London: Routledge, 1964.

Revon, Maxime. *La vie et les oeuvres de Prosper Mérimée.* Paris: Garnier, 1960.

Rousseaux, André. "Prosper Mérimée." In *Le Monde classique.* Paris: Boivin, 1927.

Sainte-Beuve, Charles Augustin. "Prosper Mérimée." In *Portraits Contemporains,* Paris: Hazan, 1863.

————. *Prosper Mérimée, mes poisons.* Paris: Pilon & Nourrit, 1869.

Saintsbury, George. *Essay on Prosper Mérimée, his Life and his Works.* London: Macmillan, 1889.

Symons, Arthur. *Prosper Mérimée.* London: Heinemann, n.d.

Taine, Hippolyte. *Étude sur Prosper Mérimée et ses Lettres a une inconnue.* Paris: Hachette, 1887.

————. "Prosper Mérimée." In *Derniers essais de critique et d'histoire.* Paris: Hachette, 1890.

Thiebaut, Marcel. *Notes sur Prosper Mérimée.* Monaco: Du Rocher, 1945.

Tourneux, M. *Prosper Mérimée: sa bibliographie.* Paris: Michel, 1876.

————. *Prosper Mérimée: ses portraits, sa bibliothèque.* Paris: Michel, 1879.

Trahard, P. *Prosper Mérimée et l'art de la nouvelle.* Paris: Gallimard, 1923.

————. *La jeunesse de Prosper Mérimée.* 2 vols. Paris: Gallimard, 1925.

Trahard, P., and Champion, E., eds. *Oeuvres complètes de Prosper Mérimée.* 8 vols. Paris: Firmin-Didot, 1927.